YOUR KNOWLEDGE HAS VALUE

- We will publish your bachelor's and master's thesis, essays and papers

- Your own eBook and book - sold worldwide in all relevant shops

- Earn money with each sale

Upload your text at www.GRIN.com and publish for free

Norman Peitek

Exploration of Competitive Market Behavior Using Near-Real-Time Sentiment Analysis

GRIN Publishing

Bibliographic information published by the German National Library:

The German National Library lists this publication in the National Bibliography; detailed bibliographic data are available on the Internet at http://dnb.dnb.de .

This book is copyright material and must not be copied, reproduced, transferred, distributed, leased, licensed or publicly performed or used in any way except as specifically permitted in writing by the publishers, as allowed under the terms and conditions under which it was purchased or as strictly permitted by applicable copyright law. Any unauthorized distribution or use of this text may be a direct infringement of the author s and publisher s rights and those responsible may be liable in law accordingly.

Imprint:

Copyright © 2014 GRIN Verlag GmbH
Print and binding: Books on Demand GmbH, Norderstedt Germany
ISBN: 978-3-656-86869-9

This book at GRIN:

http://www.grin.com/en/e-book/286583/exploration-of-competitive-market-beha-vior-using-near-real-time-sentiment

GRIN - Your knowledge has value

Since its foundation in 1998, GRIN has specialized in publishing academic texts by students, college teachers and other academics as e-book and printed book. The website www.grin.com is an ideal platform for presenting term papers, final papers, scientific essays, dissertations and specialist books.

Visit us on the internet:

http://www.grin.com/

http://www.facebook.com/grincom

http://www.twitter.com/grin_com

Otto von Guericke University Magdeburg

Faculty of Computer Science

Master Thesis

Exploration of Competitive Market Behavior Using

Near-Real-Time Sentiment Analysis

Author

Norman Peitek

24.11.2014

I. Abstract

Emotions are not only the foundation of human life, but also influence all decisions in modern markets. Grasping the reasoning behind our choices is a key element in economic sciences. Sentiment analysis, a tool to extract emotions from text, is used in this thesis to analyze customers' opinions in various markets. The calculations are done on a server architecture that is designed to be scalable for massive input directly from social networks. It computes the sentiment score in a flexible multi-stage process and provides several methods of accessing the results.

Subsequently, it is demonstrated how to use the system's capabilities by implementing various commercial use cases. This includes geographical and demographic analysis. Additionally, the system is able to provide near-real-time results.

Lastly, the thesis concludes by performing several correlation analyses on the collected data. This illustrates how the intensity of emotions vary by the maturity and form of the economic market and affects the participating companies in these markets.

II. Acknowledgements

First of all, I would express my gratitude for all the assistance I received from Prof. Dr. Reiner Dumke. Not only did he advise my bachelor thesis and master thesis, he also provided endless help in my endeavors for two adventures abroad. Furthermore, Prof. Dumke was also a reason that I received a full scholarship.

Dr. Robert Neumann guided and advised me during the course of my advancement through academia, which now finalizes in this master thesis. I feel very thankful for the inspiration, which not only steered me through this thesis, but also through the last few years.

This master thesis was primarily researched and written while I was living in Stevens Point, USA. My internship at the local university was supervised by Scott Gile, who did more than manage my work. He also encouraged, inspired, and mentored me on a daily basis. I feel extraordinarily grateful for the experience I gained that year.

Another inspiration of the last year in Wisconsin was my constant motivation from Jesse Kosobucki. Thank you for inciting me to continue to work on myself and being extremely patient through my long working hours on this thesis.

None of that would have been possible without the continuous support from my parents for the past 25 years. All of the experiences of the past, which eventually lead to this master thesis, were permitted by the infinite help I received.

Contents

III. List of Figures

IV. List of Tables

V. List of Equations

VI. Abbreviations

API   – Application Programming Interface

BI   – Business Intelligence

B2C   – Business to Consumer (Market)

HDFS – Hadoop Distributed File System

JSON – JavaScript Object Notation

POS   – Part-of-Speech

RAM   – Random Access Memory

REST – Representational State Transfer

SVM   – Support Vector Machines

VM   – Virtual Machine

1. Introduction

Humanity has come a long way in the last few thousand years. One fact stayed true throughout time: our opinions are the fundamentals for all of our activities. Our beliefs, our perceptions of the world around us, and the emotions processing that information are a key factor which set us humans apart from other living creatures. Our state of mind has and permanently will shape our lives on a day-to-day basis. Although it is such a central part of our existence, we have a hard time grasping the concept. We design and label discrete categories of emotions and feelings to better explain ourselves. However, the accuracy is thoroughly limited. If someone says he is happy, *how* happy is he? Why is he happy? Humans have a hard time quantifying and reasoning their feelings.

In the modern world, this becomes especially clear in economic markets. Our emotions are often the deciding factor of our actions in marketplaces, even though we usually pretend to argue with the facts of the product features. The decisions for—or against—a product or service are often ultimately made by our subconscious viewpoints. Understanding that behavior, and the partially hidden reasoning, would give us the opportunity to further comprehend ourselves and our actions better.

Unfortunately, it is virtually impossible to track our emotions during our day-to-day life. Luckily, we have developed languages to express ourselves. The work in this thesis endeavors to use that indirect link to our state of mind to quantify our feelings. Extracting human emotions and feelings from language, ideally text, is called sentiment analysis [1]. Later, the collected and processed data attempts to grasp our sentiments in economic markets. Overall, the work in this thesis ties multiple areas of research together: it requires computer science to design a capable server architecture and it uses knowledge from economics and business theory to analyze the results of that system. Finally, it can be further expanded into areas of consumer behavior and social sciences.

1.1. Goal of the Thesis

The goal of this thesis is to use publically available text data of consumers to understand their sentiments and behaviors in a market place. In order to be capable of evaluating customers' sentiments, a system needs to be implemented to perform natural language processing tools to extract the sentiment from a written text. Another goal of the system is to be extremely fast to achieve near-real-time results[1]. Furthermore, the system also needs to handle large amount of data. While none of the said techniques are revolutionary, the tools were never tied together into one system to achieve something unique. The complex development is structured in three technical phases, while two supplementary analysis phases exploit the system for commercial and scientific interests.

Initially, in phase one, it requires the development of a sentiment analysis system, which is close to state-of-the-art technology. The algorithm should be able to analyze and predict the sentiment of a written sentence, paragraph, or of an entire document. It utilizes a scalable algorithm, which can process substantial amounts of data.

The second phase includes the utilization of this algorithm in a large-scale sentiment analysis system. It adds components to the sentiment analysis to store the raw texts in a data storage with high-read performance. It also is able to analyze a continuous stream of incoming texts. The system should be optimized towards a source with a promising potential for a constant stream of generated user data, e.g. a social network.

The third phase is to prepare the system for further usage. This can be commercial or scientific interests. This covers the addition of high performance database querying for analytics. It also includes offering real-time monitoring of sentiment values. For the latter, the system needs to offer easy access and visual tools for exploration of variations in sentiments.

Finally, in phase four, the data of the system is used to analyze current markets and answer several customer behavioral questions. This includes attempting to understand the actions and sentiments of consumers regarding competing brands.

---

[1] Near-real-time is a "designation that pertains to the timeliness of data or information that has been delayed by the time required for electronic communication and automatic data processing. This implies that there are no significant delays" [102]

1.2. Chapter Outline

The master thesis is structured in several chapters. The first chapter Sentiment Analysis will cover the fundamental objectives, principles, and challenges of sentiment analysis. Before including several algorithmic methods of understanding sentiments of written text, it introduces a number of measures to compare accuracy. The argument for one process to be implemented in phase one will be made.

The next chapter, Large-Scale Sentiment Analysis System, covers development phases two and three. It explains how to access streams of social network data, store, and analyze them in a scalable fashion. The chapter also reasons for the choice of a specific structure to handle the scalability challenge. It additionally illustrates the steps of a high performance sentiment analysis process. In order to compare the functioning of the system, different evaluations will be made. Lastly, the system is prepared for scientific and commercial uses.

The second functionality will be exploited in chapter Commercial Use Cases: Attaining Competitive Advantages. This section implements a structured view of the data to gain new knowledge about customers and their opinions. It will also apply the near-real-time capabilities of the system to reveal current developments in economic markets.

Lastly, the system is used to attempt to gain information about consumer behavior in market situations. Several questions are articulated and the sentiment data, including the query interfaces, are used to attempt to reason for the consumers' behavior.

2. Sentiment Analysis

With the rise of information technology, the amount of documents available on digital storage is vastly increasing. While shifting from traditional paper documents to electronic data, the way humans organize their files is changing. Old-fashioned processes for filing, sorting, and finding paper documents cannot be applied to their electronic counterparts. Electronic filing has the advantage that there are numerous ways of indexing and discovering the data.

While the possibilities increased, at least at the beginning of electronic filing, individuals often sorted their documents by topic. Subsequently, since the establishment of electronic files, researchers have used machine learning techniques to automatically classify documents into categories. That was the beginning of algorithms which go through natural text, analyze, and assign a numerical or text value depending on the content. Over the years, the use cases and goals varied, but the basic idea—algorithmically understanding the content of written natural language—stayed the same. Initially, numerically quantifying the sentiment of a text was not part of the goal.

However, the last two decades saw an enormous increase of Internet use and the widespread of websites with user generated content. Content based on reviews of products, movies, or books has especially gained significant popularity. In 2002, Pang et al. [2] suggested to transfer the topic classification methods to review websites in order to automatically classify a review as positive or negative. The main goal was to produce a label or short summary of the text. Similarly and also in 2002, Turney [3] automatically applied *recommended* or *not recommended* to reviews. These were the first very basic applications of sentiment analysis.

Sentiment analysis, sometimes also called opinion mining, refers to attempting to determine the attitude and emotions underlying the text written by a human being. The term describing the research area changed over time and even today, these still are interchangeably used terms for it [4]. This thesis will use sentiment analysis.

In 2002, Turney [2] demonstrated that standard machine learning techniques can outperform human-produced baselines of understanding human emotions in movie reviews by classifying documents into a positive or negative sentiment. The authors applied a variety of different machine learning algorithms. While they have small differences in performance, they all outperform proposed classifications by humans. The overall accuracy rate for the human baseline (50% to 69%) is low [2]. This reveals the complexity of understanding natural language.

In 2004, Pang et al. [5] presented one of the first complex algorithms that "seeks to identify the viewpoint(s) underlying a text span." Again, the domain was movie reviews. For early research, the domain of movie reviews was ideal because the website requested a thumbs up or a thumbs down as a summary for the text. The classifier then attempted to predict the result by analyzing the written review.

2.1. Goals of Sentiment Analysis

Sentiment analysis goes beyond the previous examples which associate a short text with a semantic direction, i.e. either negative or positive. The classification to the negative/positive scale is a strong simplification of human emotions, which are very complex. Connecting a text to a most accurate emotion is a challenging task. The latest research tries to specify the intensity of the emotion, for example weak positive and strong positive [4].

Another goal is to understand whether the text contains polarity or not. For example, stating a fact does not contain any emotion, while announcing personal feelings unfolds the writer's emotional state. Nevertheless, emotions go beyond a positive/negative or neutral/emotional scale.

Whitelaw et al. [6] researched appraisal groups in context of sentiment analysis. The researchers additionally added the attitude (affect, appreciation or judgment) and graduation (force or focus) to orientation (positive/negative) and polarity (marked or unmarked). The combination of the four attributes allowed the research team to further understand the emotional state.

The previous goals just predict the sentiment. A further goal of sentiment analysis is to understand *why* a certain text is positive or negative. For example, a review of a smartphone could be moderately positive, because of the excellent size and battery life, but not perfect because of the low quality of the camera. Understanding contextual aspects is a difficult task, which can be very valuable for commercial applications [7].

Another area of concentration is the comparison between two entities [8]. The sentiment analysis algorithm attempts to quantity which product the user prefers based on the given text. Lastly, the last two aspects can be combined. For example, Camera A is better than Camera B, because the user likes the lighter weight, which is important to him.

Emotions are a large element of human life, but are also a not even remotely comprehensible component. Humans sometimes struggle recognizing their own emotions. Understanding the thought processes and feelings of others is not always mutually intelligible. The idea of having a neutral evaluator of an emotion, a computer algorithm, is a thought-provoking idea.

The goals of sentiment analysis developed over the years. In the first years, it was a challenge for the scientific community even though [9] predicted in 2003 that sentiment analysis has the potential for a "competitive analysis, marketing analysis, and detection of unfavorable rumors for risk management." The technology was under heavy research, but companies did not have easy access to the required data. The further increase of fast Internet access and the growing popularity of online communities started to provide a large pool of data to tap into. Product review websites provided a range of negative and positive texts. However, these were biased and a selection of human emotions. Finally, the rise of social networks offers an almost unfiltered stream of human emotions in written form.

2.2. Use Cases of Sentiment Analysis

The first applications were using sentiment analysis to classify reviews on websites and text documents. This basically can be done on any topic or domain [10]. Popular examples are hotels [11], movies [2], [12], politics [13], product reviews [14], and news [15],

[16]. Often the analysis is done in a two dimensional way—the sentiment is either positive or negative. Sometimes the polarity scale (emotional or factual) is also analyzed.

In the following years, sentiment analysis developed further uses, especially for businesses. Companies had a strong interest in measuring the user's feelings towards their products. Traditionally, this had to be done in costly surveys and it was complicated to communicate to unsatisfied individual costumers. When the Internet started to be a platform for exchanging opinions and experiences with products, a large opportunity emerged.

In the past, a complaining customer was hard to detect through classic polling and impossible to mitigate. Nowadays, if a customer complains on the Internet, the company of the product can contact the person and offer help or compensation. This can significantly improve the satisfaction and word-of-mouth.

If sentiment analysis is used to automatically classify large quantities of feedback and reviews, the company can develop many measurements of customer satisfaction. It gives them the opportunity to closely monitor and examine the sentiment of their customers. In the long run, this can be essential for any company.

Another approach for the company is to understand themes of products and markets. This can be done on multiples dimensions, not just positive or negative [17]. Summarization of reviews is another element of sentiment analysis [18], [19]. Monitoring the market also includes understanding success factors of the products from the competition.

The recent years exhibited the importance of online review platforms for users' purchase decisions. Negative reviews can significantly influence a company's success in a market. Competitors are aware of the potential to impact the market by adding fake reviews on websites. Jindal and Liu [20] researched and showed the wide-spread of "opinion spam." They also identify different kinds of spam and propose detection algorithms to countervail the effects of opinion spam.

Sentiment analysis does not have to be within a business background. Politicians, especially during election periods, are closely monitoring their success on social networks. Monitoring the change over time gives them a tool to adjust their strategies. The opportunity also attracted election prediction researcher. Tumasjan et al. [21] used Twitter as a reflection of the users' political sentiment to correctly predict the outcome of the 2010 German Election

Sentiment analysis is also a very interesting field for market research. Similar to a business, the research team can replace or complement classic polling strategies to collect data about customers' opinions. Huberman and Asur [22] shows that it is possible to predict the box revenue of movies just by listening to statuses on the social network Twitter. It requires analyzing the pre-release attention and release-phase attention to calculate the success of a movie. The research concluded that the prediction based on sentiment analysis in social networks can outperform classic polling in accuracy, time effectiveness, and costs. Another scientific discovery is that Twitter even is able to predict the stock market [23].

While the opportunities are huge, there are risks involved. An excellent example of sentiment analysis with undesired side effects is the Hathaway case. As earlier mentioned, the mood on Twitter can predict the stock market. Anne Hathaway, an actress, and Berkshire Hathaway, a company, might be a perfect show case of such a side effect. The data suggests, that whenever Anne Hathaway is in a positive way in the news, the Berkshire company stocks went up [24]. This is a correlation which could be caused by automatic trading software on the stock market, which indicates that the software takes sentiments on social networks into account.

The various use cases demonstrate the need for a precise calculation of users' sentiment. There are a few challenges to calculate the sentiment value of a written text. The next chapter will introduce several aspects of the complexity of processing natural language.

2.3. Challenges of Processing Natural Language

As described in an earlier section, sentiment analysis attempts to fulfill a variety of use cases by achieving several aspects of recognizing sentiment in human language. This is a very difficult task. Language is very imprecise and contains several aspects which can strongly change or even reverse the meaning of an entire paragraph. Humans use these linguistic devices to express themselves more strongly. Additionally, written text is a very noisy area [25]. An entire article can state hundreds of sentences which just objectively state facts and do not have any subjective sentiment and then one sentence can change the entire, overall sentiment.

The sentiment analysis algorithm needs to differentiate between facts and opinions, and also understand how strong these opinions are. However, emotions do not have to be stated directly. Humans can express themselves by using negation, irrealis, or sarcasm. This chapter will explore several features of human language. It explains why it is difficult to detect these aspects and possibly how to mitigate troublesome characteristics of human language.

2.3.1. Negation

One of the most important linguistic devices is negation. Language negators (i.e. "*not,*" "*without,*" and "*lacks*") reverse the polarity of a sentence and are a complicated detail of sentiment analysis. The following excerpt from a movie review [26] demonstrates the power of negators:

This film should be brilliant. It sounds like a great plot, the actors are first grade, and the supporting cast is good as well, and Stallone is attempting to deliver a good performance. However, it can't hold up.

The quote features several clear-cut positive words and a single imperceptible negator reverses the entire sentiment of the review. Negation is a very powerful tool in the human language, but extremely hard to detect and understand for algorithms [27]. Research agrees that they play an important role in the overall accuracy [28], [29].

However, the main goal of this master thesis is the analysis of overall sentiment value of a company's brand in a specific time frame. The individual sentiment of a single text is less critical, since there is an aggregation of thousands of sentiment values into one score. Thus, the negation—in this specific use case—is of less impact, because it will overall offset when aggregating the sentiment values. Nonetheless, in the future it is necessary to add a negation analysis module.

Another variation of negation is sarcasm or irony. That is "classically defined as the rhetorical process of intentionally using words or expressions for uttering a meaning different (usually the opposite) from the one they have when used literally" [30]. Detecting irony is possible, if emoticons (see section Emoticons, Acronyms, and Further Improvements) or ratings are used which have the opposite meaning of the text [31].

2.3.2. Deontic Irrealis

Deontic irrealis is a linguistic term for describing a failed expectation or desire. This is particularly difficult to detect and score in the sentiment analysis process. For example:

"This movie should have been good."

This sentence has *"good"* as an indicator for positive sentiment and no direct pointers for a negative sentiment [4]. However, the sentiment of the writer is towards the negative side, since his high expectations have not been met and he thus holds a negative sentiment of disappointment.

2.3.3. Languages

So far, one important factor regarding sentiment analysis was ignored—language. Throughout the world, there are a variety of languages that are represented on the Internet, which is data source of this master's thesis. Depending on the used algorithm, the transfer to another language could be in different forms. The supervised machine-learning classifiers need to be trained on a new dataset. If the system uses a dictionary-based approach, an entire new dictionary needs to be created for the language. Parts of some algorithms are based on language features which are specific to Western languages.

Most research has been done on Western languages, especially English. These languages have high similarities in syntax and grammar. Asiatic languages, for example, have a significantly different syntax and require a vastly modified implementation of the sentiment analysis algorithm. The Chinese language, with vastly different language syntax and word constructs, has been researched successfully [32].

Ideally, the system will be multilingual by design. Denecke [33] and Hiroshi et al. [34] accomplished this by automatically translating reviews to English and then running sentiment analysis on the translated text. Bautin et al. [35] used a similar approach to compare the different reactions to world news in nine societies. However, this system is limited by the quality of the machine translation and the amount of sentiment becoming lost in the translations.

Boyd-Graber and Resnik [36] implemented a multilingual supervised latent Dirichlet allocation, which results in a "probabilistic generative model that allows insights gleaned from one language's data to inform how the model captures properties of other languages." This is the foundation to make sentiment analysis algorithms work across languages. Abase et al. [37] implemented an actual system to work with English and Arabic forum posts. Even though the languages are fundamentally diverse, they reached a common accuracy over both languages of over 90%. However, human communication goes beyond the use of words, independent of the used language.

2.3.4. Emoticons, Acronyms, and Further Improvements

Generally, non-verbal expressions are lost when using written communication. Yet, humans can attempt to replace facial expressions and moods via emoticons. Emoticons are "graphic representations of facial expressions" [38]. An example selection sorted by frequency of use is viewable in Table 1 [39].

Emoticon	Meaning
:-)	smile, happy, positive
;-)	wink, joking, positive
:-(	frown, sad, negative
:-D	wide grin, happy, funny, positive
:-p	tongue sticking out, joking, positive
:'(	crying, sad, negative

Table 1 – Emoticons and Their Meanings

Unlike words, emoticons have low ambiguity in their sentimental meaning. Thus, they are an excellent opportunity to improve the classification precision of a sentiment algorithm. Past research proves that the consideration of emoticons in texts can improve the results [39], [40].

However, the use of emoticons is not the only change of language featured when humans communicate via written words. People have formed a whole new subset of terms. One element is the extensive use of acronyms, especially by replacing phonetic sounds by numbers with the identical phonetic sound. Table 2 provides examples. Aue and Gamon [40] reassigned acronyms into their original meaning and achieved positive results.

Acronym	Word, Meaning
gr8, gr8t	great
Lol	laughing out loud
Rotf	rolling on the floor
Bff	best friend forever

Table 2 – Acronyms and the Corresponding Words

The scientific community did not stop at these obvious chances to further improve the accuracy. The human language offers many aspects to learn the meaning with a machine. An example is the understanding of target-specific adjectives by Fahrni and Klenner [41] or added adverbs by Benamara et al. [42].

2.4. Domain-specific Language

The previous sections were very general and based on language granularities. However, humans tend to use a different type of language depending on the domain. Even if the algorithms understand the words and syntax correctly, the result can vary between various topics. The majority of sentiment classification algorithms are supervised and directly or indirectly based on a dictionary—an association of word(s) to a positive or negative meaning. These dictionaries are often built to a specific domain to accomplish the highest possible outcome. If the text data source is shifted into a different domain, where another type of language is used, a significant drop in accuracy is observed [43].

Taboada et al. [4] show that movies, which are based off of video games, are largely not well received. When a reviewer mentions the word "game," it is often a strong negative indicator, but this only applies for movie reviews. In other domains, the word "game" is just noise without a particular sentiment.

When shifting the domain, the previously used training data could render partly or completely inoperable. Building the dictionary or a training set is the largest factor of effort when implementing a system to run sentiment analyses. If it is required to build a completely new dictionary for every domain, the effort multiplies. One approach is to use the training data from the previous domain and to transfer it to the new domain [44]. Another approach is to have one large training set instead of many smaller but separated ones. Aue and Gamon [40] investigated combining the dictionaries of the various fields—books, movies, and electronics—while maintaining the level of accuracy. The last chapter clarified how challenging sentiment analysis is. In order to be effective, the algorithm needs to be accurate and low on errors. The next section introduces several algorithms and approaches to conclude human emotions from text.

2.5. Algorithmic Principles of Sentimental Analysis

The last sections motivated and reasoned for concentrated research in sentiment analysis. While the configuration for the diverse use cases can be unique, the main component is the algorithm, which processes the natural language and calculates a numerical value for the chosen scale. Due to the essentialness of this component, the majority of past research focused on developing and testing approaches. Sentiment analysis generally is considered a topic of machine learning and thus inherits a collection of algorithms.

Nevertheless, research did not limit to proven machine learning algorithms. A variety of diverse methods were analyzed and examined. In order to truly compare different approaches, the researchers relied on traditional success measurements from information retrieval: precision and recall. The next section will provide a brief introduction to typical measurement scales of natural language processing.

2.6. Measuring Sentiment Analysis Accuracy

When implementing sentiment analysis algorithms, as with any system for information retrieval, the algorithms need to be evaluated by a comparable measure. One approach is using the confusion table to calculate precision and recall.

Confusion Table		Sentiment Analysis Prediction	
		Positive	Negative
Actual Sentiment	Positive	True Positive	False Negative
	Negative	False Positive	True Negative

Table 3 – Confusion Table

2.6.1. Precision, Recall and Accuracy

Precision is computed with the help of the confusion table and the following formula:

$$\rho = \frac{|True\ Positive|}{|True\ Positive + True\ Negative|}$$

Equation 1 – Computation of Precision

Recall is calculated with this formula:

$$r = \frac{|True\ Positive|}{|True\ Positive + False\ Negative|}$$

Equation 2 – Computation of Recall

Precision and recall are usually dependent of each other. Systems can aim to achieve an excellent value in one measurement, while suffering a lesser value in the other. One approach to combine the two scales into one is accuracy, which will be described next, or the F-score, which is described in the next section.

Accuracy is defined as:

$$Accuracy = \frac{|True\ Positive| + |True\ Negative|}{|Positive\ Tweets + Negative\ Tweets|}$$

Equation 3 – Computation of Accuracy

2.6.2. F-score

F-score, or also described as F-measurement, simplifies precision and recall into one scale. The computation uses the following formula:

$$F_\beta = (1 + \beta^2) \frac{\rho r}{r + \beta^2 \rho}$$

Equation 4 – Computation of F-score [45]

Using Equation 1 – Computation of Precision and Equation 2 – Computation of Recall, the F-score is computed as:

$$F_\beta = \frac{(1 + \beta^2)\ True\ Positive}{(1 + \beta^2)\ True\ Positive + \beta^2\ False\ Negative + False\ Positive}$$

Equation 5 – Computation of F-score with Confusion Table

The balanced F-score, sometimes referred as F-measurement or F_1score, is simplified. It is the harmonic mean of the precision and recall. The F-score represents a perfect value at 1 and the worst value at 0. Its formula is:

$$F_1 = 2 \frac{\rho r}{\rho + r}$$

Equation 6 – Balanced F-score

While the predication of precision, recall, and F-score are questioned due to biases and subjectivity [46], researchers still publish their papers with precision and recall numbers. Currently, two main approaches are considered state-of-the-art with high precision. The next two sections will give an overview over the functions and advantages.

2.6.3. Supervised Machine-Learning Algorithms

As mentioned in an earlier section, the beginning of sentiment analysis was in predicting the numerical values of ratings for product reviews. Common patterns are either a
positive/negative rating or a one to five star rating, which easily can be converted to a
positive/negative rating. The algorithm now had to classify a review, which is text, to a
two alternative classification. This is very similar to the existing text classification problem, i.e. applied to categorization of text. Therefore, the existing approaches and algorithms were used for initial sentiment analysis via machine learning methods.

One of the first papers in the sentiment analysis research area used supervised algorithms, namely Naives Bayes and SVM (Support Vector Machines), to classify movie
reviews into a positive/negative classification with equivalent success. The challenge of
sentiment analysis is that only a few words of a text can be strong indicators for the sentiment, or even shift the sentiment (see Challenges of Processing Natural Language).
The simple supervised algorithms do not take that uniqueness into account. Thus, researchers developed specialized features for sentiment analysis.

Nevertheless, the basic approach remains constant. The classification algorithm requires
some classified dataset to train the classifier and then apply it to the unknown, new dataset. The exact algorithm is interchangeable. Researchers also proved the effectiveness
with Maximum Entropy analysis and logistic regression [47], [48].

The overall disadvantage is that classification algorithms are usually trained towards a
specific topic. Sentiment is expressed by a few strong indication words, which can vary
depending on the domain of the text. If the classifier needs to cover a wide range of topics, it can be less accurate. If the classifier is specialized for a small area, the training
will not result into successful uses outside of that area. Unsupervised algorithms are a
solution to that problem.

2.6.4. Unsupervised Algorithms

The appeal of unsupervised algorithms is clear in the fast setup and easy domain transfer. However, since particular words are often the indicator and foundation of sentiment

analysis, not having a training dataset makes this approach particularly difficult to implement.

Turney [3] demonstrates a multi-step-algorithm using part-of-speech (POS) tagging, calculation of point wise mutual information, and the average over all phrases in the review. The overall effort and accuracy was not as prosperous as desired. There are more techniques for unsupervised algorithms using the common knowledge of single words. The next section will describe successful methods.

2.6.5. Dictionary-based Algorithms

A different unsupervised approach to sentiment analysis was successful: dictionary or lexicon-based algorithms [4], [49]. The idea is simple: the text to be classified is divided into either single words or a bag of words and each part requests a lookup in a sentiment dictionary, which contains information about the strength (weak or strong sentiment) and direction (negative or positive sentiment) of the word. If the word is not in the sentiment dictionary, a regular dictionary is used to find synonyms—or antonyms—which are in the sentiment dictionary and use their score, or respectively the negative of it in the case of an antonym. The sentiment value of the text is a simple summation of the sentiment value of each word [43].

The advantage of the dictionary-based algorithms is the simplicity and speediness of the calculation. The system only needs a few known sentiment indicator words to classify a text. The task also can be parallelized for scalability, either on word or text basis. The supervised machine-learning techniques always require the entire text to evaluate the sentiment score, while the dictionary-based algorithm can divide the text into multiple sections and calculate each segment separately.

The evaluation algorithm generally works the following way:

"This excellent car is a lot of fun."

The sentence would be broken up into smaller parts, for example, for unigrams:

Unigram	This	excellent	car	is	a	lot	of	fun	Score
Objectivity	n/a	0	1	n/a	n/a	1	n/a	0.625	0.65
Polarity	n/a	0.75	0	n/a	n/a	0	n/a	0.375	0.56

Table 4 – Demo for Calculating Sentiment Scores

The last column in Table 4 displays the final score for that sentence. The objectiveness score is at 0.65, which is less than 1. Thus it is a sentence which reflects personal opinion and emotion, and not just stating a fact. The sentiment is clearly positive, since the polarity is a positive numerical value of 0.56. Therefore, the writer expresses a positive sentiment.

The algorithm used in the table is a simple lookup to the SentiWordNet dictionary [49]. The dictionary provides values for objectivity, positivity, and negativity. For an easier scale, the positivity and negativity is combined into one polarity value. The objectivity scale goes from 0 (complete emotional statement, no factual information) to 1 (pure fact, no emotions). The polarity is a scale from -1 (very negative sentiment) to +1 (very positive sentiment).

The objectivity is calculated by adding all existing numbers together and then dividing it by the amount. Words which have "n/a" as the value are ignored. Mathematically, the formula can be expressed the following way:

$$Sentiment\ Score_{Objectivity} = \frac{\sum_{k=0}^{n} \alpha(word_k)}{n}$$

Equation 7 – Sentiment Score Objectivity

with

$$n - amount\ of\ words$$

$$\alpha - SentiWordNet\ function\ to\ look\ up\ objectivity\ score$$

The polarity score is calculated similarly:

$$Sentiment\ Score_{Polarity} = \frac{\sum_{k=0}^{n} \beta(word_k)}{n}$$

Equation 8 – Sentiment Score Polarity

with

n − $amount\ of\ words\ where\ objectvitiy\ is\ not\ 1$

β − $SentiWordNet\ function\ to\ look\ up\ subjectivity\ score$

This is only one calculation method. There are several versions of this approach, which fine-tune or change parts of the process. Additionally, many extensions adjust the sentiment value after taking additional calculations into account. The basic score is calculated on a word-basis, as described above. Then the value is adjusted down or up depending on additional measurements. For example, how the words relate within a sentence or within paragraphs [5].

To conclude, the largest disadvantage of this approach is that the success highly depends upon the quality of the dictionary. This requires an extensive amount of work to build such a dictionary. Ameur and Jamoussi [50], and Kanayama and Nasukawa [51] present methods how to dynamically build and update sentiment dictionaries to mitigate the issue. This can be particularly useful if the system is used in a certain domain. Supervised classifiers can train to have the correct sentiment interpretation of a word. A dictionary generally has the common sentiment which can be the opposite in a domain. A "small" TV has a rather negative sentiment, while a "small" camera is viewed positively. The supervised classifier would be trained for each domain and thus correctly calculate the sentiment of "small".

Batool et al. [52] demonstrate on a sentiment analysis system how to dynamically add a keyword-based knowledge extractor. The extracted word knowledge can be further enriched and outperforms standard systems.

2.6.6. Comparison of the Sentiment Analysis Algorithms

The research team of Andreevskaia and Bergler [53] implemented both general approaches and compared the results. Both algorithm classes have different, opposite strengths and weaknesses. The dictionary-based implementation performs very well on the Pearson-correlation (sentiment assigned by algorithm versus the human annotation), the ternary accuracy, and the binary precision (negative/positive). It does have a very low recall. On the other hand, the Naives Bayes algorithm has a much higher recall, but has lower scores in the other categories. Table 5 displays the numerical results.

Approach	Pearson-correlation	Accuracy	Precision	Recall	F1
Dictionary-Based	47.7	55.1	61.4	9.2	16
Naives-Bayes	25.4	31.2	31.2	66.4	42

Table 5 – Result Comparison between Sentiment Algorithms [53]

While the exact scores are different, the overall success is obtainable with both approaches. The difference in implementation is the test or scoring database. The dictionary-based approach requires a large dictionary of scored unigrams. The Naives Bayes algorithm requires a large learning dataset (at least 500 [53]) to have a sufficient classification model. There are multiple free sentiment dictionaries available, but the training dataset has to be manually classified for each topic.

Finally, it is possible to combine the previously mentioned algorithms. Prabowo and Thelwall [54] implement a semi-automatic combination of multiple algorithms which complement each other. The results are an enhanced accuracy, but also a considerably increased complexity.

All approaches have almost indistinguishable differences in their overall success. If correctly set up and trained, every algorithm achieves excellent results. After experimenting with a tf-idf (term frequency–inverse document frequency) classifier, a dictionary-based algorithm was the best choice for this master thesis. It was not possible to obtain enough labeled test data to successfully train a statistical algorithm on various topics.

Another important aspect is the scalability and speed of the calculation. The machine learning tools had problems to give near-real-time results with the amount of stream data from social networks. Also, it is difficult to parallelize the sentiment evaluation process.

Lastly, the dictionary-based algorithm in addition gives the opportunity to divide the scoring process into multiple steps and thus gain preliminary fast estimations (see Scheduling and Modularity for Near-Real-Time Predictions). Following, revised sentiment scores are applied as the complex algorithms are being computed.

2.7. Sentiment Analysis in Social Networks

As mentioned in the introduction, social media is an important source of opinion data in recent years. There are many active social networks nowadays: Twitter, Facebook.com, Reddit.com or Blogger.com. Twitter has been the focus point of past sentiment analysis research in social media [55] due to the possibility of accessing almost all data. Even more popular websites, like Facebook, have a very restricted access to the statements of their users due to privacy strategies. Twitter is designed for everything to be public. Moreover, Twitter has an open API to access the social data in a structured form (see also Twitter's Streaming API).

Social data is the data generated by human activity on social online networks. Since online networks became so popular, accessing the data can be valuable for scientific and commercial purposes. While social networks already play an important role in today's business decisions and marketing, analyzing the user's sentiment is unexploited. That is surprising, since Twitter was compared to online word-of-mouth branding [56].

Huberman and Asur [22] point out that the large potential of social media data is largely untapped. However, the scientific community around sentiment analysis started to focus on social media and made significant discoveries. An advantage of social networks is the availability of additional data due to the structure, e.g. demographic information, circle of friends, and online activity. One successful example exploiting this opportunity is the team of Tan et al. [57], who discovered that users, who are in a social relationship, tend to hold similar opinions by relating the results of sentiment analysis on Twitter.

Twitter is a special case of social networks. Unlike others, the texts are limited to 140 characters and thus very short. While this is favorable from a storage and processing speed perspective, it makes the sentiment analysis aspect even harder. Since 140 characters limit the expression to one or a maximum of a few sentences, many algorithms cease to apply [53]. Additionally, the prediction of the sentiment based a very small dataset (140 characters) is naturally less accurate than an entire essay (product review). Furthermore, unlike movie reviews, there is no direct indicator for providing training data [58].

However, when working with aggregated values, the accuracy for a specific tweet becomes less significant, because multiple inaccuracies will be offset overall [59]. As Pak and Paroubek [59] illustrate, all social network analysis systems have one disadvantage: the massive amount of data. In order to have a chance to manage the amount of data, the algorithms need to prioritize speed over preciseness. The next chapter will discuss and reason for software solutions to process the data.

3. Large-Scale Sentiment Analysis System

As shown in the introduction, analyzing data from social networks can be very beneficial and has various potential use cases. Yet, very few technical implementations exist, whose purpose are one-time scientific analyses and which operate on historical data. The reason for the scarcity of such continuing systems is the technical challenges of big data. Big data is defined as "high-volume, high-velocity and high-variety information assets that demand cost-effective, innovative forms of information processing for enhanced insight and decision making" [60], [61]. Social networks have been classified as big data sources [62]. The system thus has to mitigate multiple challenges at once: handling a big data source and attacking the sentiment analysis problem.

The goals of the system implemented in this thesis are two-fold. First, it takes on the challenge of managing the immense data stream from social networks. While less challenging sources might exist, they do not have the appeal of the authenticity of social data. Second, the system should not just generally be able to handle the data, it should also provide (preliminary) results very quickly. Although historical sentiment values have their application, providing sentiments near real-time unlocks another set of opportunities.

Additionally, the system needs to resolve several technical issues. Firstly, it needs to handle the technical challenges of scraping the data from social networks. Secondly, it needs to store that data in a high-performance database with fast reading capabilities. Thirdly, after the most complex part—the sentiment computation—it needs to provide aggregated values for further analysis and information processing.

3.1. System Architecture Overview

As outlined, the system has several components to it. The social network data goes through several stages. This process is linear, because the steps cannot be parallelized and are interdependent. This information path, with the according general system architecture, is illustrated in Figure 1.

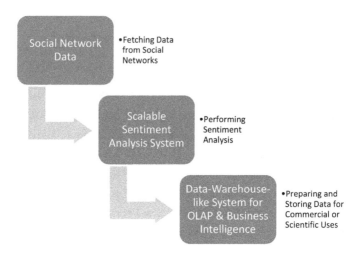

Figure 1 – Designed Process for a Large-Scale Sentiment Analysis System

3.2. Data Scraping

In most big data use cases, it is a company analyzing its own data to gain insight about customers, production efficiency, or security. However, in this use case, the data from social networks is required. Social networks differ in their level of privacy and generally the thoughts and opinions of every user are not accessible. For example, Facebook.com limits their access to intentionally public posts. This is a very small percentage of all posted data and not sufficient to obtain an accurate estimate of the user's sentiment.

Better suited candidates are Twitter.com or Reddit.com. Both networks are set to post publicly by default. This means all content is anonymously viewable. They also provide this data by their APIs [63], [64]. Twitter is a better candidate due to their concept. Twitter is a micro-blogging service, where people can post their opinion, thoughts, or feelings limited to 140 characters. While discussions are possible, everything stays in a linear format. Reddit, on the other hand, is organized in forums and has a nested style. This makes it much more difficult to analyze the discussions.

Twitter is a very promising candidate for a large-scale sentiment analysis system. The content produced by more than 271 million monthly active users [65] gives enough leverage to implement and thoroughly test such a system. Before the analysis is possible, the system needs to pull the data.

Ideally, the system would not just use one source. Combining many sources into one system and merging the results would achieve the best result. This would compensate for possible imbalances between the different networks. Unfortunately, it would greatly increase the complexity of the overall system architecture. While the sentiment analysis of text is primarily similar (besides different text lengths), the access to the text varies according to the social network. This is due to the fact that every network uses a different data structure for their data. The system must have the ability to work with any of the diverse data structures or to find a uniform structure. Both would be possible, but beyond the scope of this master thesis.

3.2.1. Data Structure

As described in the previous section, there are multiple options to gather data. The advantage of social networks which offer APIs is that they return structured data. Structured data follows a clearly pre-defined data model where the meaning of each part is known.

Due to the reasons of accessibility and fixed structure, Twitter is the chosen source of data. The essential parts of Twitter's data are the "tweets" which represent one message of a user. A tweet may only be 140 characters long. The tweet text is not the only part of the data model which is returned by Twitter's API. In the next section, how the developed system can access the tweets is described in the next section.

3.2.2. Twitter's Streaming API

Twitter offers REST APIs to access their data and to interact with the service. For this use case, only their streaming API, which provides a real-time stream of all tweets for a specific search query, is needed. The streaming API forwards all tweets to a registered listener depending on their filtering settings. Twitter does not allow gathering all tweets due to the size of data created and the value of that complete data stream. The search criteria, mainly one or more keywords, need to be known a-priori.

Additional filters are offered, but only one more is used for this system: language. Twitter automatically detects the language of a tweet. It is possible to filter for a specific language. In this case, only tweets in English are gathered and analyzed. This is another decision to make the sentiment analysis system less complex. In further work, a multilingual system should be developed.

Figure 2 visualizes the architecture of Twitter's streaming API. The sentiment analysis server registers at Twitter's server and continuously listens to incoming tweets. If the server falls too far behind or the connection is lost, the streaming ends. Otherwise the streaming is a continuous process.

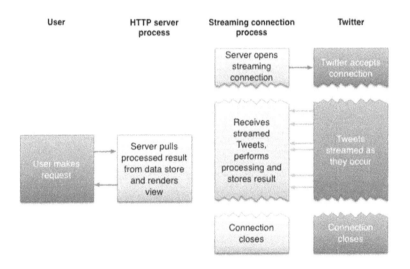

Figure 2 - Twitter's Streaming API [66]

For the server used in this master thesis, it was necessary to listen to multiple keywords and thus fetch a large amount of tweets about various keywords in the English language. In order to showcase the capabilities in the later chapters, it was necessary to collect data in different categories of economic and social markets. The gathered stream, which is collected over time, will be used for the later applications in the chapters Commercial Use Cases: Attaining Competitive Advantages and Scientific Use Cases: Understanding Competitive Market Behavior.

The data analyses are focused on three different economic markets. The reasoning behind choosing these markets will be explained in the later chapters. The first market is the young, very competitive market of smartphone operating systems. Table 6 presents the used keywords.

	Keyword	Language
1.	Android	English
2.	iOS	English
3.	WindowsPhone	English

Table 6 – Search Keywords for Smartphone Manufacturer Market

A theoretically very similar area, the competition among computer operating systems, might result in completely different results due to the difference in maturity and market composition. Table 7 lists the used keywords for the collected data in the computer operating systems.

	Keyword	Language
1.	MacOS	English
2.	Windows	English
3.	Linux	English

Table 7 – Search Keywords for Computer Operating Systems

Finally, a diverse market is chosen for the last marketplace. Table 8 specifies keywords to analyze the market for German premium car brands.

	Keyword	Language
1.	BMW	English
2.	Mercedes	English
3.	Audi	English

Table 8 – Search Keywords for Premium German Car Manufacturers

Additional, further analyses will be made to examine smaller effects. However, these will be explained in the according sections. The main focus of the analyses is on these three markets. All three tables feature keywords with high popularity, and thus need an efficient system to handle the data.

Any technology, which is able to do HTTP connections, can register with the Twitter API. However storing and processing that data is much more demanding. Due to the characteristics of big data sources, the system needs to have very potent capabilities. The next section will describe a possible solution.

3.3. Scalability with Hadoop

Once again, one of the main challenges is the pure size of data. Twitter users can be very active. A prominent example is the reported peak during the final of the Euro Cup 2012. Over 15,000 tweets per *second* were being sent [67]. Furthermore, it is not just the peak; it is also the overall mass of data for a day.

Receiving, storing, and analyzing the data requires a very powerful machine. As shown by the tweet per second peak example, it needs to be extraordinarily scalable as well. Two possible approaches would be a potent supercomputer like IBM Watson [68] or advanced in-memory computing like SAP Hana [69]. Both would be able to handle the amount of data and have the required computing power to run sentiment analysis. However, they are also very expensive and do not scale well.

Hadoop is being developed by the Apache Foundation and offers a scalable, cost-effective, and powerful solution. Unlike the previous suggestions, which scale up, Hadoop scales out. This means instead of using an even more powerful machine, it adds another piece of commodity hardware to the cluster [70]. The required storing and analysis tasks are distributed to child parts of the cluster and then globally aggregated.

3.3.1. Scalable Data Storage: HDFS and HBase

The system mainly needs two scalable parts: computation and data storage. The computation is done by MapReduce jobs, which will be explained in the next section. The Hadoop ecosystem offers many options for data storage, but the system implemented in this thesis is going to utilize two wide-spread options. Both have equally high performance in write and read operations. The Hadoop Distributed File System (HDFS) is a distributed file-system, which is able to operate with high input and output by utilizing a large amount of commodity machines.

HBase is built on top of HDFS. HBase is a non-relational distributed database, which specializes in handling sparse data. It performs especially well when searching for a few samples from a very large dataset [71]. This is especially interesting for searching the storage of an entire incoming stream of tweet data. A practical example would be to query for all the tweets within the area of Magdeburg, Germany. This might only be dozens in a dataset of millions of tweets, but these sparse data scenarios are one of the strengths of HBase.

Storing millions of tweets, or in later version of the system any structured social media data, is one challenge. Yet, more important, especially for near-real-time results, is the scalability and fast computation of sentiments. The next section will introduce the concept of MapReduce, which fulfills the need for scalable computation.

3.3.2. Scalable Computation: MapReduce and Derivatives

The scalable computation uses an algorithm called MapReduce, which was developed by two Google engineers in 2004 [72]. MapReduce is "a programming model and an associated implementation for processing and generating large data sets" [72]. It processes data in two steps: Map and Reduce.

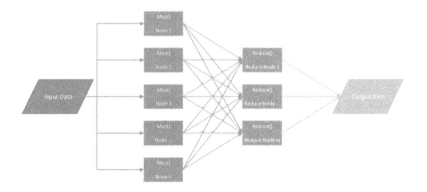

Figure 3 – Composition and Basic Principle of MapReduce

Figure 3 displays the functionality of MapReduce. MapReduce distributes the mapping tasks to all available nodes. Each node is computing data on its own. There are no inter-dependencies between the mapping nodes. However, all mapping nodes split the computation results and then pass the grouped results each to different reduce nodes. The reduce nodes have to wait for all map nodes to be finished with the calculations until the final result is completed. The system has the large advantage of being very scalable. If the computation task becomes more complex and it can be evaluated in a MapReduce algorithm, Hadoop's MapReduce offers a powerful solution. If the processing takes too long, the administrator can add more commodity machines to increase the computation power and shorten the algorithm running time.

There are disadvantages as well. MapReduce and Hadoop do not handle the loss of nodes while running computations well. The performance regarding the fastness of the calculation is also poor. MapReduce requires a lot of communication between the nodes. It only outperforms common machines when handling a large amount of data. In the case of this master thesis, there is a lot of computation intense language processing. While the solution does not provide real-time capabilities by analyzing streams of data, it does offer scalable processing. This is the major accomplishment of the architecture. In order to analyze millions of tweets simultaneously, there is a larger requirement to be scalable than to be fast.

In summary, there are concepts and technologies to complete massively scalable data storage and computation. There are also existing tools to complete sentiment analysis and query social network data. The next section will introduce the design of an architecture, which ties everything together for an operational prototype.

3.4. Sentiment Analysis Implementation

Sentiment analysis researchers have primarily focused on accuracy of the language processing, rather than the speed or scalability of the solution. However, Godbole et al. [16] presented an early work on scalable systems. It is large-scale, but not actually scalable for linear-like growth. It requires a powerful machine for the algorithm, which consequently can handle large amounts of data. The disadvantage is that it scales up more than it scales out.

Liu et al. [73] presented a scalable sentiment classification method. The approach utilizes the Naïve Bayes classifier for completing the natural language processing. However, it was missing the aspects of optimizing the system towards near-real-time results and preparing the data for later analysis.

The system developed in this thesis had multiple goals:

- Capable of scaling out
- Comparatively fast processing to provide close to near-real-time results
- Optimize speed over accuracy without disregarding accuracy
- Preparing the results for online analysis and business use cases

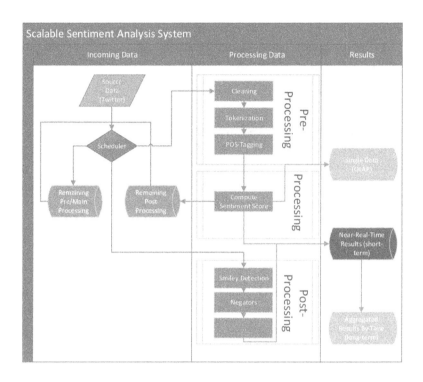

Figure 4 – Server Architecture of Scalable Sentiment Analysis System

Figure 4 above illustrates a high level overview of the developed architecture. It has an abstract split into three phases. The left side, Incoming Data, scrapes the data from APIs and schedules the processing. The scheduler decides which incoming data, in this case tweets, and moves into the next processing batch. It has the ability—if the server load is becoming too high—to push back data to the "Remaining Pre/Main Processing" storage. The data in this storage will not be touched until the server load is so light that it can compute the live incoming data in addition to the deferred data. This should especially be possible at night.

The processing queue itself transitions into the second phase, Processing Data. It is divided into three child stages. The pre-processing does the necessary work to actually run the sentiment scoring algorithm in the main processing stage. The post-processing does not directly follow. Instead, the computed data returns back to the scheduler into separate storage for remaining post-processing datasets. It also writes the results into the result sections, which features three different data storages.

The result phase enables various analyses of the data. One of the goals was to have near-real-time data available. Thus, there must be a provider for the results of the recent minutes and hours. OLAP and aggregation by time storage are more long-term oriented. These two offer access to the data for actions, which are not time sensitive.

Lastly, the scheduler has to plan the post-processing data when there is time available. This step is not critical, since the preliminary results of the sentiment scorer of the main processing step are already provided. Consequently, it has the lowest priority. This is also mandatory, because the list of post-processing steps, which increase the accuracy of the sentiment scoring, can become long. However, these algorithms should not be neglected, since they deliver a more comprehensive result.

This section described the high level architecture of the system. Further detail about each step in the process will follow in the next sections. The scraping of the data was previously explained in the chapter Data Scraping and is not a technical issue. Thus, the next section will clarify the necessary steps to complete sentiment scoring on data from Twitter.

3.4.1. Overview of Data Computing Process

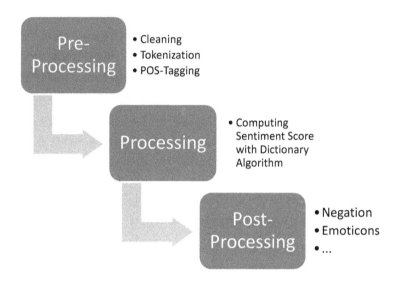

Figure 5 – Overview of Sentiment Scoring Process

In the following sections, the process of computing the sentiment score for a text will be examined. Figure 5 illustrates the overall process. Initially it was planned to be a continuous process, but due to the computation runtimes, it was split up into two parts. The process in Figure 5 is only theoretical and not the linear procedure of the technical implementation.

The procedure itself computes for each tweet a sentiment score. This sentiment score indicates how the author feels about a certain topic. Nonetheless, having a score for a single tweet is fairly useless. It is the aggregation of the score of thousands of tweets, which provides the actual value for the user of the system. Later in this thesis, the system will be used to evaluate certain markets. The data will be aggregated as well. In order to have meaningful measures for the aggregation, the system uses several algorithms to compute various scales. This enables reports and analyses to view the larger picture in the business section and provides additional information for the scientific uses section.

The most important measure is the average sentiment score. The algorithm itself produces the result for an individual tweet on a -1 to 1 scale, with -1 being a very negative sentiment and 1 being a very positive sentiment. The -1 to 1 scale is not as meaningful for businesses as a 0 to 100 scale. Thus, the -1 to 1 scale will be directly converted to the 0 to 100 scale when aggregating the sentiment score of all tweets.

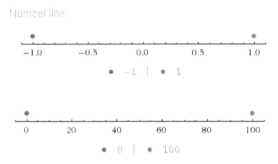

Figure 6 – Converting Single Tweet to Aggregated Sentiment Score[2]

Haberman and Asur [22] introduced two additional scales to further evaluate the sentiment of a market. The first scale is the subjectivity, which indicates how large the portion of tweets with strong emotion is:

$$Subjectivity = \frac{|Positive\ and\ Negative\ Tweets|}{|Neutral\ Tweets|}$$

Equation 9 – Tweet Aggregation Scale: Subjectivity

The second scale, which is implemented as well, is the polarity. The polarity compares the size of the two emotional states, negative and positive, with each other:

$$Polarity = \frac{|Positive\ Tweets|}{|Negative\ Tweets|}$$

Equation 10 – Tweet Aggregation Scale: Polarity

[2] Images were created with Wolfram Alpha [104]

37

3.4.2. Pre-Processing: Cleaning, Tokenization and POS-Tagging

As explained at the beginning of this thesis, extracting sentiment from written text is not an easy task. One of the issues is the noisiness of the data. Consequently, some cleaning steps are required before completing the actual scoring to achieve a precise result. The cleaning step includes the removal of all irrelevant characters to reduce the text to the expressive part. This includes the removal of links, user names, numbers, and empty spaces.

Theoretically, at this point, the sentiment scoring algorithm could start. However, since the system was designed to use a dictionary-based approach, there are two additional steps which greatly enhance the sentiment scoring precision. The used database, Senti-WordNet, does differentiate words for their position within the sentence. This method, also called part-of-speech, increases the accuracy of the stored information about the word [74]. Since part-of-speech recognition can be an entire topic on its own, the system will use a state-of-the-art algorithm by OpenNLP [75].

This part-of-speech recognition algorithm requires the text to be tokenized. Fortunately, OpenNLP provides this algorithm as well. When these three steps—cleaning, tokenization, and part-of-speech tagging—are completed, the actual sentiment scoring in the main processing stage can begin.

3.4.3. Processing: Computing the Basic Sentiment Score

The Sentiment Analysis chapter provided information about different algorithms to calculate the sentiment score of a text. It also reasoned for the choice of using a dictionary-based approach. Once again, instead of developing a brand new system, the implementation will use an existing state-of-the-art algorithm based on SentiWordNet [49], [33].

The algorithm itself is as simple as described at the beginning of this chapter. Each tweet was cleaned from unnecessary information, tokenized, and the parts-of-speech were tagged. Next, each token will be run against the large list of words in the Senti-WordNet database. This provides all of the necessary elements to compute the sentiment score (see Dictionary-based Algorithms).

On the one hand, the aggregated results are folded by the chosen time span and stored in the near-real-time database. This database only provides one line for each time span and contains no information about individual tweets. On the other hand, the individual results go into a separate, much larger data warehouse for later access.

3.4.4. Post-Processing: Enhancing Sentiment Analysis Score Precision

As explained in the architecture section of this chapter, the post-processing does not directly follow the main processing stage. It is a separate computing job, which might get pushed into the queue shortly after, or even a day later. The advantage of running additional algorithms is to further enhance the precision of the scoring. Dictionary-based algorithms are weak on several language aspects, such as negations or sarcasm. The goal of the post-processing stage is not to provide more accurate near-real-time results; it is designed to have better results for later OLAP analyses and reports. The data can also be used for other sentiment algorithms, i.e. product feature evaluation. It is essential to gain the most accurate sentiment score as possible. Another aspect is that with further research insights, more algorithms can extend the post-processing stage. The additional algorithms will further adjust the initial sentiment score.

In order to demonstrate the purpose of this stage, the system added a negation detection algorithm. The post-processing stage also includes an algorithm, which adjusts the sentiment if the tweet contains emoticons. Emoticons are a strong indicator for sentiment, even if they are not based upon words.

The results of the post-processing stage are deferred to the results databases for further usage. The post-processing stage might be triggered with a significant delay of time. This is caused by the different needs the scheduler must satisfy. The next section will explain the reasoning behind the multi-stage system.

3.4.5. Scheduling and Modularity for Near-Real-Time Predictions

As illustrated earlier, it is a challenge to compute a large amount of data very quickly. Doing all three tasks, pre-, main, and post-processing, in one process is too time consuming, especially when implementing more complex and precise algorithms in the future. In order to have a good foundation for future extensions, the process was split. The separation quickens the process, but simultaneously increases the complexity of the scheduling. The post-processing job has a very low priority, since the only reason for it is to further increase the accuracy of the sentiment score of individual tweets. The pre-processing and main processing task has to be done first, because one of the goals is to be near-real-time and the goals of the thesis value speed over accuracy. If the pre-processing and main processing jobs take up too many resources, the post-processing is stopped completely until the server capacity utilization is stabilized again. Nonetheless, pausing the post-processing is not enough to handle the possible massive input from social networks.

One of the characteristics of social networks, and this is especially true for Twitter, is peaks of activity. Within minutes, the created data can centuplicate. Pausing the post-processing can mitigate the effects of a suddenly multiplied input, but this will not be enough in peak situations. However, installing an excessive server cluster only in order to handle peaks is a waste of resources, since they will be not utilized a large percentage of time. Consequently, the scheduler also limits the amount of tweets going to the queue, if a peak situation occurs. Depending upon the capacity of the server cluster, the limit is currently set to an arbitrary number. If the queue is filled up and the previous computation job is not yet complete (a typical situation in a peak scenario), the incoming data goes into a separate temporary database. The next computation job will be flagged as sample and not entirely calculated. When the server cluster has free capacities again, the tweets in the temporary database have the next-highest priority to be processed. The scheduler is at this time reasonably simple. Future iterations should improve the scheduling. However, this would go beyond the scope of this master thesis. To conclude, the scheduler has three priorities:

1. Currently Incoming Data
2. Temporarily Buffered Data (if queue was filled up previously)
3. Post-Processing

While this aids the scalability of the system, it does not promise precise results. The next section will assess the sentiment scoring itself.

3.5. Evaluation of Sentiment Analysis Accuracy

In order to evaluate the implementation of the process regarding the sentiment scoring, 500 tweets of two keywords were chosen to be tagged manually. The tagged tweets were then compared to the results of the algorithm. Next, the accuracy (see Measuring Sentiment Analysis Accuracy) was calculated. The results are viewable in Table 9.

Keyword	Accuracy
iOS	63.1%
Audi	66.9%

Table 9 – Evaluation of Implemented Sentiment Scoring Algorithm

The implemented algorithm does not reach the level of the most recent state-of-the-art research. There are several causes for the lower accuracy. First, the source is Twitter, which provides texts of no longer than 140 characters and is often shaped by colloquial language. Due to the incomplete sentences, slang, and inattentive writing, the diction-ary-based approach misses more than it usually would with movie reviews or other more sophisticated texts. Second, the dictionary was not further adapted to the domain of smartphones or premium cars. Most dictionary-based research uses adjusted diction-aries and not general-valid ones like SentiWordNet. This results in less accurate scoring, but also keeps the domain-transferability very high. The system should not be limited by focusing on one domain. The goal is to be able to use any topic or keyword on Twitter for analysis purposes. Lastly, due to the focus on other areas, only two post-processing algorithms were implemented. Most state-of-the-art research uses more complex ap-proaches, e.g. inter-sentence sentiment adjusters. Nevertheless, with the modular archi-tecture described in the previous sections, these algorithms can easily be added to im-prove the post-processing accuracy.

Overall, the need for very precise scoring is relatively low. At least with Twitter as a source, it will be very hard to achieve much higher results. Additionally, the main use for the system is to aggregate the sentiments of individual tweets for an overall keyword sentiment score. The individual accuracy can be lower, since it will be offset when ag-gregating a vast number of tweets. More important is that the large number of tweets can be processed. The next section will evaluate the system's capabilities regarding the speed and scalability.

3.6. Evaluation of Speed and Scalability

The implementation was completed with the pre-packed QuickStart Hadoop VMs (Virtual Machine) from Cloudera [76], which provides a working setup with many helpful tools. This chapter presents selected results from timing different computation steps. This illustrates why the architecture had to be divided into a modular scheme.

Task	Required Time	Summation
Scheduling/Job Start	16.4s	16.4s
Cleaning	12.1s	28.5s
Tokenization	7.7s	36.2s
POS-Tagging	31.2s	107.4s
Sentiment Scoring	23.6s	131.0s
Scheduling & Database Overhead	31.4s	162.4s
Result		~Two Minutes 42 Seconds

Table 10 – Pre-Processing and Processing: Computation Times

Table 10 shows the measured times for each step of the pre-processing and main processing. The measurement was done with a job of 30,000 tweets, which would cover approximately five to six hours for a keyword with mediocre popularity. The overall computing time of two minutes and 42 seconds is reasonably fast, especially since this is done on a VM with one processor and just two Gigabytes of RAM.

The second step, the post-processing is completed afterwards. While currently there are only two executed algorithms, the list could grow considerably in the future.

Task	Required Time	Summation
Scheduling/Job Start	3.8s	3.8s
Negation	19.2s	24s
Emoticons	15.7s	39.7s
Scheduling & Database Overhead	24.2s	63.9s
Result		~One Minute 4 Seconds

Table 11 – Post-Processing: Computation Times

Table 11 lists the measured times to complete the post-processing for the same 30,000 tweets. Obviously when considering the measured times, running the processing for multiple popular keywords could be difficult on a single machine. Therefore, the server needs to be extended in order to be a cluster. This was easily done, since Hadoop is designed to run as a cluster. As expected, when running the process on multiple VMs, the calculation times for the post-processing decreases.

	Single VM	Two VM	Three VM
Computing Time	63.9s	52.5s	48.6s
Difference (based on Single VM)	n/a	-17.84%	-23.94%

Table 12 – Decrease in Computation Time with Added VMs

The significance of this test is limited. The computation was not run on an actual server cluster. Instead, it was run on the emulated Hadoop cluster from Cloudera. The percentage difference and drop are expected to be larger on a real cluster. Nevertheless, even with the emulated cluster, a clear drop in computing time can be observed. Figure 7 below illustrates the decrease in processing time.

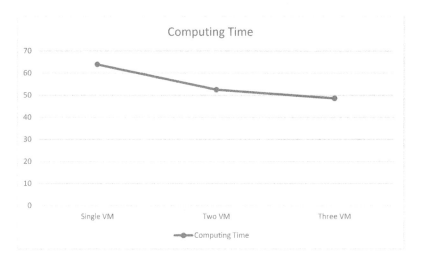

Figure 7 – Decrease in Computation Time with More VMs

3.7. Providing Results – Using the Calculated Sentiments

At this point, the capabilities of the initial vision of the system are implemented. The system can perform a sentiment analysis on large quantities of structured data from social media sources. It is designed to process for fast results, while also being as exact as possible. However, so far, the sentiment scoring results have not been used. This section will outline several possible aspects of using the data and designing data structures, which can perform well for the required specifications.

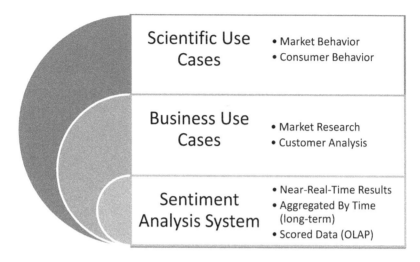

Scientific Use Cases	• Market Behavior • Consumer Behavior
Business Use Cases	• Market Research • Customer Analysis
Sentiment Analysis System	• Near-Real-Time Results • Aggregated By Time (long-term) • Scored Data (OLAP)

Figure 8 – Potential and Use Cases of the Sentiment Analysis System

The next step is to design an architecture, which provides the result in a fashion desired by the clients. Figure 8 visualizes the potential use cases. Each has a diverse need for the provided data schema. The next two sections will describe the approaches to provide the results of the system.

3.7.1. Aggregated Sentiment Values and Near-Real-Time Analysis

The aggregated values from a configurable time span can be very interesting for scientific research and partly for commercial use cases.

Date Start	Date End	Average Sentiment	Tweet Count	Processing Complete	Post-Processing Complete
15/10/2014 14:05	15/10/2014 14:10	65.2	942	Yes	Yes
15/10/2014 14:10	15/10/2014 14:15	70.4	704	Yes	No
15/10/2014 14:15	15/10/2014 14:20	63.5	900	No	No

Table 13 – Database Design for Aggregated Sentiment Values

The database for near-real-time analysis only provides limited information in order to be very fast. The database schema includes time, average sentiment, tweet count, a flag if the processing is complete, and lastly a flag if the post-processing is complete. Table 13 shows three sample rows of the design database schema.

Businesses might be even more interested in the pure, but scored, tweet data for more complex queries. The next section will introduce a concept called online analytical processing.

3.7.2. Preparing for Basic Online Analytical Processing

Online analytical processing (OLAP) is a set of technologies to serve multi-dimensional data for querying, business mining, and reporting [77]. The pure, non-aggregated, and scored social data can be viewed as multi-dimensional. Especially eligible as dimensions are geolocation (since Twitter often provides this information), time, and sentiment score. Designing, providing, and running a data warehouse for online analytical processing is a challenge on its own and goes beyond the scope of this master thesis. Thus, the data warehouse section of the system would not be ready for real-world practice.

However, the potential usage still applies, since access to the pure, but scored, Twitter data can be very valuable. Enhancing the data warehouse capabilities is an issue of development time rather than a research question. This is particularly true, since the dimensions can grow once there are more sources added. For example, if the system would also acquire data from Facebook, the profile information like gender, age, or residence location can create another dimension. However, the system so far only uses data from Twitter and provides the following dimensions:

- Search Keyword
- Time
- Geolocation
- Sentiment Score
- Polarity
- Subjectivity
- Tweet Count

While this is not a fully balanced data warehouse with exhaustive OLAP tools, it provides enough resources to utilize it for a few sample applications. The next chapter Commercial Use Cases: Attaining Competitive Advantages will present several use cases for the aggregated sentiment values, near-real-time data, and also the OLAP capabilities.

4. Commercial Use Cases: Attaining Competitive Advantages

Companies invest heavily into their marketing and customer research capabilities. They create studies, ask clients for their opinions, and closely monitor the customer lifecycle to analyze the success and failure of their products. The disadvantage of this process is that it is costly, time-consuming, and might delay the gain of important information.

With the rise of the Internet and the implementation of customer reviews, it became significantly easier to access customers' sentiment of products. However, analyzing user reviews can be an inaccurate sample of the overall sentiment. The users who are motivated enough to dedicate their time to write an online review without a financial reward might be positively or negatively biased. Additionally, product reviews on ecommerce websites often also reflect the experience with a particular merchant. For example: a customer receives a product late, due to shipping problems. The customer may give the product a bad review because it was very late, even though it does not reflect the qualities of the product itself.

4.1. Business Brand Value Monitoring

Nowadays, a large percentage of consumers, especially in the Business-to-Customer (B2C) market, inform and express themselves about products online [78]. Tapping into the data, which is unconsciously expressed and not mindfully published onto a review website, provides the business with the potential to gain new knowledge. In order to acquire this knowledge, the business requires the data and necessary tools available. The system implemented in this master thesis can be used for such a purpose. This chapter introduces several uses of the system for commercial interests.

4.1.1. Near-Real-Time Monitoring

Monitoring the unfiltered stream of posts on social media has a different set of challenges, but one key advantage. Unlike most other methods, this can be near-real-time. The system described in the previous chapter enables the company to collect important information about their brand and products. The technology has the aptitude to display the current numerical sentiment value, the latest trend, and potential quick changes. The system databases already have the (possibly preliminary) information calculated and stored. The final missing piece is a software component to display the information. Figure 9 displays an implementation to view the current development and latest changes within the last hour of the sentiment score and the overall tweet count.

Figure 9 – Visualization of Sentiment Score and Volume

The screenshot also shows how the modular analysis system makes a difference. The black line indicates a finished calculation with all post-processing algorithms. A dashed line signals a completed basic sentiment algorithm, however the post-processing algorithms must still be completed for a more exact result. Finally, the dotted line reveals that the basic sentiment analysis is only partly concluded. In other words, the sample processing is currently running and the results might change quickly. Overall, the dashboard gives the company a tool to closely monitor the changes in their customers' sentiment.

It is not necessary for an employee to watch the dashboard every minute of every day. Notifications can be setup which alarm the (marketing or customer relationship) employee in configured situations, e.g. a significant drop (or gain), or if the sentiment falls below a certain threshold. Also, the number of tweets per time unit can be an indicator for extraordinary events. A company who uses this dashboard and the alarm system exploits the power of the system and has a substantial competitive advantage. They are able to notice a change in customer satisfaction very quickly. This makes it possible to counteract or to minimize the negative impact.

An example scenario is the following: an ecommerce company sells products online. Due to a technical problem in the specific payment provider, some consumers cannot pay and finish their order. At this point, customers would be confused and may or may not call customer service. The company possibly will notice the problems from incoming calls, but it will also leave some customers unsatisfied. When online users are encountering technical difficulties, they often share their problems online. If the company uses the dashboard, it will see the drop in their average sentiment within the last few minutes and can investigate the problem quicker. When they conclude that the problem is an external factor, they can communicate the root source of the problem and suggest an alternative payment solution. The customer will reflect the bad experience on the payment provider and not the ecommerce company. Monitoring the social media sentiment of the customers has helped to prevent a drop in customer satisfaction by quickly counteracting the problem.

4.1.2. Historical Analysis

The usage is not only limited to near-real-time reactions. The system, depending upon the setup time, furthermore provides aggregated historical sentiment values. After some time, the company can also exploit this knowledge base. One question that is always relevant for businesses is if the customer satisfaction is improving. With a historical view of the data, for example in Figure 10, the overall trend can be displayed in the last months or years.

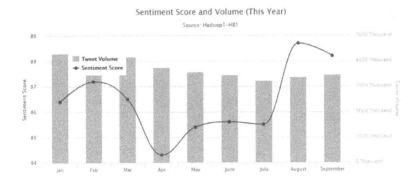

Figure 10 – Historical View of Sentiment Score and Tweet Count

Large fluctuations in a short time might have a previously unknown cause. A press report might have positively or negatively impacted the customers' sentiment. The visual
tool helps to recognize possible sentiment factors. Analyzed scores can be grouped by
any time span, for example, months. Pie charts are a popular solution to visualize the
strength of each section. Figure 11 demonstrates such a pie chart, which groups the sentiment score by the month of September and by the positivity of the score.

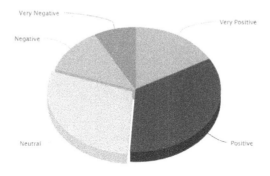

Tweets by Sentiment Score, September 2014

Very Negative
Very Positive
Negative
Neutral
Positive

Figure 11 – Pie Chart of Tweets by Sentiment Score (Monthly Summary)

The usage of the aggregated data does not necessarily need to be a graphic implementation. Numerical numbers, which summarize the development, can be provided for executive reports. Colorful indicators can additionally signal the development. The Figure 12 showcases such a report.

Sentiment Status Report

Overall Status: **At Risk**

Brand Name: iPhones

September 14, 2014

Status Code Legend

- On Track: Excellent Sentiment Value
- At Risk: Good Sentiment Value, but decreasing
- High Risk: Low Sentiment
- Off Track: Significant Loss in Sentiment, Very Negative Mood

The project is **AT RISK** the week of 9/15/2014 - 9/21/2014, due to the following:	● The count went up to 422,586 tweets for the last 7 days ● That is a plus of 9,3% over the previous week ● The sentiment score declined slightly by 1.3 points
Issues:	● New Samsung S5 was presented last week and drew a lot of attention ● The Unlock-Security Bug was highly publicized and drew the largest negative sentiment

Figure 12 – Sentiment Score Executive Report

Expanding on the idea of executive reports: time is not the only interesting axis of the data matrix. While social networks do not necessarily always provide exact information, the additional information besides the text itself can be used for further analysis.

4.1.3. Demographic and Geolocation-based Analyses

Almost all businesses segment their products and customers by various factors, e.g. age, financial capabilities, or location. The system implemented in this master thesis is based on data from Twitter, which does not include real names (for age analysis) or job titles (financial situation). It does very often include the precise location of the sent tweet. If the system was fed from a different social network or multiple sources, more factors could be used for advanced demographic analysis. However, since twitter only reliably provides location data, the next sections will use this information to showcase how to gain more knowledge about customers.

Separating the customer by location can be very interesting, especially for international or expanding companies. An example is a company which is debating expansion into different areas or countries. Usually, products are known und reviewed in other countries before the official rollout. If the company knows in which countries the sentiment toward their product is the highest, it can be an important factor in decision making. Another usage is the knowledge where products are viewed positively (or negatively), which improves sales and customer satisfaction by precise use of segmented marketing tools. Identical products can be viewed very differently depending upon the customers' culture. Dixon et al. [79] analyzed the sentiment of various fast food chains across different continents. The results are as expected: the fast food chains have vastly different sentiment values depending upon the customers' location. Even single products provoke distinctly different reactions in very close locations. With this knowledge, the company can carefully design marketing strategies to improve the sentiment in specific regions.

Region	Product	Sentiment Score	Overall Tweet Count (in Thousands)	Region Rank for that Product
Europe	Smartphone	74.5	320.44	#2
	Tablet	64.2	96.80	#3
North America	Smartphone	73.1	328.82	#3
	Tablet	76.9	153.41	#1
Asia	Smartphone	80.4	460.38	#1
	Tablet	73.0	174.03	#2

Table 14 – Sentiment Scores by Region and Product

Since the data is already stored and prepared in the system, it can be queried and grouped by location. A new aggregation method then computes averages by time and location. As demonstrated by Table 14, the system can illustrate this information in a comprehensible way to aid decision-making.

Another option, instead of a tabular view, is to overlay the data directly on the map. This could be a geographical heat map of negative or positive thoughts. Furthermore, the map could also display the tweet count in order to recognize strong areas.

Figure 13 – Heat Map of Tweet Count for a Business in Melbourne

For example, a business might want to know where people are talking about their brand and products. Figure 13 demonstrates a heat map of tweets around the city of Melbourne, Australia. This can be a very potent tool for any commercial or non-commercial units to analyze customers.

Similarly, other demographic criteria could be very interesting. If the premium car brand has a positive overall sentiment on the Internet, the results might be very misleading for the company. The overall sentiment value is heavily influenced by—on average—a younger audience. However, the younger audience generally cannot afford the car and thus the opinion of the target customer segment, middle-aged or older men, is much more relevant. Through tapping into the data of a social network, which directly or indirectly provides age information, the sentiment values can be segmented and the company can achieve a much more relevant value.

Monitoring and examining the trend of the sentiment values of a company's brand or products does not require an implementation of further algorithms. Although the website for the screenshots above was implemented on the JavaScript environment node.js, HTML, and the interactive JavaScript charts framework Highcharts [80], the technology is irrelevant. It is simply a view of the existing information on databases. Any programming language or software, which can connect to databases or APIs, can use the information the system collects. Moreover, the pool of raw and aggregated data can be used for further scenarios.

56

4.2. Sentiments of Brands, Products and Markets

Thus far, only the business brand or a single product was discussed. However, the system is not limited to one product. Most companies have several products, which vary in their success. While sale and profit are good indicators of the state of a product, the sentiment score offers another tool to further understand the market situation. The sentiment score comparison is especially important when a company has a set of products and has to decide which ones should be further supported, developed, or even retracted from the market. The business should not purely make the decision on the financial success in the past, but also the potential the product holds in the future. This system can provide key indicators, the recognition, and sentiment score for each product of the business. As already mentioned, the data can be viewed in different ways to drill down to the knowledge to aid decision making.

Figure 14 – Average Sentiment Score (Monthly) for Multiple Products

Figure 14 demonstrates a competitive comparison between three products. Product B is clearly their highest performer. The tool helps to visualize that Product A and Product C are becoming closer and closer in their sentiment score. At the beginning of the year, Product C was the superior product. However, the trend clearly goes towards Product A. Without considering the opposite sentiment score development in the last months, the company might have made the wrong decision.

The sentiment scores, in combination with traditional financial information, can assist the business to make the right decision and to survive competitive market situations. Keeping in mind that the information analyzed is public information, any business could also examine the sentiments of their competitors. The market analysis enables the company to see beyond their own situation and to look at the entire market. Most companies are not located within a monopoly market and have to consider the success and possible failure of competitive products. This system provides a tool to better understand the market. However, counting the tweets and averaging the sentiment might not be enough to understand the reasons of a certain sentiment.

4.3. Sentiments of Product Features

Another popular sentiment analysis approach is to examine the cause of a positive or negative sentiment. Which feature or problem of the product builds the foundation for a negative sentiment? What are attributes that lead to a positive sentiment about the product? There has been research about feature-aspects of sentiment analysis [14]. However, it was limited to offline one-time analyses.

The base system described in this thesis has the capability to run the algorithm for sections of the past and evaluates the changes over time. A feature, which might be a cause for a positive sentiment in the past, can change to a negative sentiment. Previously, small mobile phones were considered as the best. Currently, smartphones tend to be larger, due to the increasing screen sizes which are growing because of customers' demands. Understanding the changes of customers' needs over time is an essential key to the long-term survival of a company.

In order to run the algorithms for feature-aspects of sentiment analysis, the base data is required. The system already collects the social media stream information (in this case, tweets) and stores them in databases. The algorithm now performs on a selection of the data. The process to identify the sentiments of product features has four steps [14]:

1. Identify product features
2. Identify opinions regarding product features
3. Determine the polarity of opinions

4. Rank opinions based on their strength.

Relevant Product Features for Sentiment Category (August 2014)

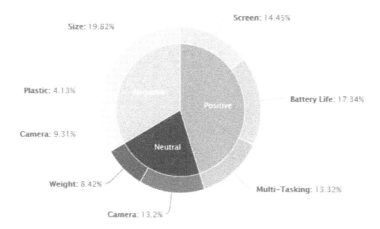

Figure 15 – Pie Chart of Relevant Product Features for Sentiment Category

The results can be illustrated by using a similar visual tool as show in the previous section. Specialized views for the gained knowledge are possible as well. Figure 15 does not only illustrate the strength of sentiment categories for a product, it also narrows down for the specific features. If the company can understand which features are causing a positive (or negative) sentiment, they are able to improve the next product release specific to the customers' needs.

Once again, companies that begin to monitor the customers' sentiment of their product features will gain a competitive advantage. They can understand if certain features are a good or bad element. Businesses can observe how it changes over time and react quicker and more precisely than their competition.

Understanding processes in business markets can help companies survive and expand their economic position. Similarly, observing these processes from an outside perspective with minimal interference can be very interesting for economic and social sciences.

The same system, which provides companies with tools, can be expanded to a larger scale and can monitor entire markets with multiple companies. The next chapter will present attempts to scale the system from a single business to an economical level.

5. Scientific Use Cases: Understanding Competitive Market Behavior

The previous chapter focused on using the system for the business interests of a single company, their brand, and products. Despite the fact that it can be very useful for a business, the system's capabilities are not limited to a commercial use. If the system is setup to gather information about an entire market with multiple companies and a multitude of products, there might be more scientific research analyses possible. This chapter will examine a few hypotheses based upon the results of sentiment analyses of entire market situations.

Previous research has shown that posting reviews online can affect an entire market [26]. This influence reflects how important online communities are nowadays to the economy. The framework of the developed system permits first-hand market research which is close to the customers. Before the results are compared, the next section will introduce fundamental market theory and some used market classifications.

5.1. Fundamentals of Economic Markets

An economic market is "a place where products are bought and sold" [81]. Markets can vary in numerous variables. Consequently, economists developed several classifications to separate diverse types of markets. In this thesis, the data of two classification types is analyzed for patterns and new insight.

5.1.1. Market Forms

Microeconomics, which focuses on the behavior of individuals and participants of the market, introduces multiple stages of markets depending on their strength of competition [82]. Based on the data collected previously, the work in this thesis is limited to three types of competitions.

Monopoly is a market where a single seller has the exclusive possession of the supply [82]. One of the markets the system collected data from is the computer operating system market with primarily three players: Microsoft's Windows, Apple's Mac OS X, and various Linux derivatives. Although there are multiple sellers of the product, the market is still classified as a monopoly due to the dominant market share of Microsoft's Windows, high entry barriers, and the necessary investments for potential new competitors [83].

A different market is the smartphone market with the key competitors of Google's Android, Apple's iOS, Microsoft's Windows Phone, among others. Due to the market share and the success of Android and iOS, this market is classified as a duopoly [84]. A duopoly is a situation where two suppliers dominate the market [82].

Lastly, the premium car brands represent an oligopoly [85] due to the relatively even market share and distributed market power. To conclude, the collected data covers three distinct classifications of markets. Nevertheless, the distribution of power between the suppliers is not the only measure to categorize a market.

5.1.2. Market Maturity

For economists, market maturity is less of a relevant factor. In this thesis, however, it is a very interesting viewpoint. There are four stages of market maturity [86], [87]:

- Stage 1. Survival
- Stage 2. Quality
- Stage 3. Convenience
- Stage 4. Customization.

There does not appear to be peer-reviewed sources, which classify either one of the analyzed markets into one of the maturity stages. Nonetheless, based upon the factors presented in the source material, the categorization is straightforward. Table 15 summarizes the classifications.

	Market Form	Market Maturity
Smartphone Operation Systems	Duopoly	Stage 1/Stage 2
Computer Operation Systems	Monopoly	Stage 3
Premium Car Manufactures	Oligopoly	Stage 4

Table 15 – Classification of the Analyzed Markets

5.2. Sentiments in Competitive Markets

After categorizing the collected data into various markets types, this section will take a closer look at the relationships between the competitors. One common expectation would be that if the sentiment of Company A goes down (i.e. users complain), the sentiment of the competing Company B goes up. This belief sounds reasonable, because customers often argue with the problems of the opposing business. The next section will examine the first hypothesis.

5.2.1. First Hypothesis

- H1: There is a correlation of the sentiments between competitors in the same Market.

In order to compute the correlation, we will use the collected data from January 1st, 2014 until September 30th, 2014. Based upon the gathered tweets, a sentiment score for each day was computed. This results in a dataset of 271 points for every search keyword. For each set and market, the Pearson product-moment correlation coefficient [88] and the Kendall rank correlation coefficient [89] are calculated. The processing is done with Wessa.net, an online free statistic software [90].

Premium Car Market

The first market is the premium car market. The collected data is from BMW, Mercedes, and Audi. All three share a roughly equal market share and similar market power.

Pearson Product Moment Correlation – Audi and BMV		
Statistic	Variable X (Audi)	Variable Y (BMW)
Mean	73.9264705882353	66.3382352941177
Biased Variance	105.391652249135	68.6282439446367
Biased Standard Deviation	10.2660436512385	8.2842165558752
Covariance	1.15780334273931	
Correlation	**0.0135637768510468**	
Determination	0.000183976042464994	
T-Test	0.222896101102961	
p-value (2 sided)	0.823784901589857	
p-value (1 sided)	0.411892450794928	
Kendall tau Rank Correlation		
Kendall tau	-0.0187808685004711	
2-sided p-value	0.657646954059601	
Score	-660	
Var(Score)	2211268.5	
Denominator	35142.14453125	

Table 16 – Absolute Sentiment Score – Correlation between Audi and BWM

Pearson Product Moment Correlation – Mercedes and BMW		
Statistic	Variable X (Mercedes)	Variable Y (BMW)
Mean	64.9411764705882	66.3382352941177
Biased Variance	38.3347750865052	68.6282439446367
Biased Standard Deviation	6.19150830464639	8.2842165558752
Covariance	-0.323203820273497	
Correlation	**-0.00627811070264474**	
Determination	3.94146739946625e-05	
T-Test	-0.103161918577322	
p-value (2 sided)	0.917911043779745	
p-value (1 sided)	0.458955521889873	
Kendall tau Rank Correlation		
Kendall tau	0.0138191087171435	
2-sided p-value	0.747576475143433	
Score	481	
Var(Score)	2224395	
Denominator	34806.875	

Table 17 – Absolute Sentiment Score – Correlation between Mercedes and BWM

Pearson Product Moment Correlation – Audi and Mercedes		
Statistic	Variable X (Audi)	Variable (Mercedes)
Mean	73.9264705882353	64.9411764705882
Biased Variance	105.391652249135	38.3347750865052
Biased Standard Deviation	10.2660436512385	6.19150830464639
Covariance	-4.01172129368353	
Correlation	**-0.0628827569609508**	
Determination	0.00395424112301001	
T-Test	-1.03531811023516	
p-value (2 sided)	0.301446751185489	
p-value (1 sided)	0.150723375592745	
Kendall tau Rank Correlation		
Kendall tau	-0.0311078447848558	
2-sided p-value	0.467378854751587	
Score	-1086	
Var(Score)	2228891.25	
Denominator	34910.80859375	

Table 18 – Absolute Sentiment Score – Correlation between Audi and Mercedes

The correlations, independent of the chosen correlation coefficient, are very low and vary around 0. The strongest relationship is between Audi and Mercedes with a negative correlation of -0.06 (Pearson) or -0.03 (Kendall). This is a negligible magnitude. To summarize, there appears to be no correlation between the absolute sentiment values in the market of premium cars. The premium car market hints towards the rejection of the first hypothesis.

Computer Operating System Market

Next, the second market to be examined is of computer operating systems. Here, the three competitors are Windows, Mac OS X, and Linux.

Pearson Product Moment Correlation – Windows and Linux

Statistic	Variable X (Windows)	Variable Y (Linux)
Mean	63.3198529411765	67.1102941176471
Biased Variance	23.3057823313149	39.3848940311419
Biased Standard Deviation	4.82760627343561	6.27573852475881
Covariance	2.03470262643803	
Correlation	**0.0669120982594146**	
Determination	0.00447722889347756	
T-Test	1.10194757069739	
p-value (2 sided)	0.271465778072562	
p-value (1 sided)	0.135732889036281	
Kendall tau Rank Correlation		
Kendall tau	-0.102357774972916	
2-sided p-value	0.0200809091329575	
Score	-3452	
Var(Score)	2203466.5	
Denominator	33724.84375	

Table 19 – Absolute Sentiment Score – Correlation between Windows and Linux

Pearson Product Moment Correlation – Windows and Mac OS X

Statistic	Variable X (Mac OS X)	Variable Y (Windows)
Mean	56.2794117647059	67.1102941176471
Biased Variance	51.4292820069204	39.3848940311419
Biased Standard Deviation	7.17142119854359	6.27573852475881
Covariance	5.91002821792924	
Correlation	**0.130833774267778**	
Determination	0.0171174764891519	
T-Test	2.1684576539975	
p-value (2 sided)	0.0309971659913442	
p-value (1 sided)	0.0154985829956721	
Kendall tau Rank Correlation		
Kendall tau	-0.0344920381903648	
2-sided p-value	0.435924530029297	
Score	-1155	
Var(Score)	2193977.75	
Denominator	33485.98828125	

Table 20 – Absolute Sentiment Score – Correlation between Windows and Mac OS X

Pearson Product Moment Correlation – Mac OS X and Linux

Statistic	Variable X (Mac OS X)	Variable Y (Linux)
Mean	56.2794117647059	67.1102941176471
Biased Variance	51.4292820069204	39.3848940311419
Biased Standard Deviation	7.17142119854359	6.27573852475881
Covariance	5.91002821792924	
Correlation	**0.130833774267778**	
Determination	0.0171174764891519	
T-Test	2.1684576539975	
p-value (2 sided)	0.0309971659913442	
p-value (1 sided)	0.0154985829956721	
Kendall tau Rank Correlation		
Kendall tau	0.0568916127085686	
2-sided p-value	0.196329355239868	
Score	1917	
Var(Score)	2198933.5	
Denominator	33695.65234375	

Table 21 – Absolute Sentiment Score – Correlation between Mac OS X and Linux

Similar to the premium car market, the correlations are low. Nevertheless, the correlations tend to be slightly higher than the premium car market. The correlations themselves are partially unanticipated. For example, Linux and Windows are two contrary concepts for operating systems. One is proprietary and a commercialized solution by Microsoft, while Linux is a free and open source operating system. Yet, they are marginally positively correlated. Overall, due to the differences in the Pearson and Kendall correlation numbers and the unexpected positivity of the correlation, the computer operating system market hints towards the rejection of the first hypothesis as well.

Smartphone Operating Systems Market

The last market with data available is the smartphone operating systems market with the main competition between iOS and Android. A small player in the market is Microsoft's Windows Phone.

Pearson Product Moment Correlation – Android and Windows Phone		
Statistic	Variable X (Android)	Variable Y (Windows Phone)
Mean	76.3088235294118	66.3014705882353
Biased Variance	35.9119809688581	36.8576448961938
Biased Standard Deviation	5.99266059182882	6.07104973593478
Covariance	4.66301280659865	
Correlation	**0.127697831738063**	
Determination	0.0163067362306026	
T-Test	2.11560973395873	
p-value (2 sided)	0.0352936862838811	
p-value (1 sided)	0.0176468431419405	
Kendall tau Rank Correlation		
Kendall tau	0.103090852499008	
2-sided p-value	0.0168040990829468	
Score	3566	
Var(Score)	2223168.25	
Denominator	34590.84765625	

Table 22 – Absolute Sentiment Score – Correlation between Android and Windows Phone

Pearson Product Moment Correlation – iOS and Windows Phone		
Statistic	Variable X (iOS)	Variable Y (Windows Phone)
Mean	82.1985294117647	66.3014705882353
Biased Variance	62.7105860726644	36.8576448961938
Biased Standard Deviation	7.91900158306995	6.07104973593478
Covariance	1.33107228131105	
Correlation	**0.02758467083481**	
Determination	0.000760914065064817	
T-Test	0.453434939068064	
p-value (2 sided)	0.650599790583913	
p-value (1 sided)	0.325299895291957	
Kendall tau Rank Correlation		
Kendall tau	0.0583896599709988	
2-sided p-value	0.178440690040588	
Score	2004	
Var(Score)	2215890.75	
Denominator	34321.14453125	

Table 23 – Absolute Sentiment Score – Correlation between iOS and Windows Phone

Pearson Product Moment Correlation – Android and iOS

Statistic	Variable X (Android)	Variable Y (iOS)
Mean	76.3088235294118	82.1985294117647
Biased Variance	35.9119809688581	62.7105860726644
Biased Standard Deviation	5.99266059182882	7.91900158306995
Covariance	24.063924462774	
Correlation	**0.505215576026756**	
Determination	0.255242778260046	
T-Test	9.61947238183612	
p-value (2 sided)	0	
p-value (1 sided)	0	
Kendall tau Rank Correlation		
Kendall tau	0.294857949018478	
2-sided p-value	0	
Score	10246	
Var(Score)	2224579	
Denominator	34748.9375	

Table 24 – Absolute Sentiment Score – Correlation between iOS and Android

The smartphone operating systems market paints a similar image to the previous markets, with one exception. The correlation towards Windows Phone as the outsider of the duopoly is as low as the correlations in the premium car market. However, between the two main competitors in the duopoly, Android and iOS, there is a noticeable correlation of 0.51 (Pearson) and 0.29 (Kendall).

Overall, the correlations within the three markets were remarkably low. Consequently, this leads to a rejection of the first hypothesis. Only one competing pair had a significant correlation. It is not clear if this is a special case between these two companies or a result of the different types of markets. The market type disparities will be evaluated after studying more data.

Nonetheless, it leads to the consideration that perhaps directly correlating the absolute sentiment scores is not the correct approach. Possibly, correlating the change in sentiment between time spans would lead to a clearer picture. This thought process is expressed in the second hypothesis.

5.2.2. Second Hypothesis

- H2: The sentiment towards Company A moves oppositely, when company B's sentiment goes up or down.

Premium Car Market

The same dataset as the first hypothesis is used. However, instead of using the absolute sentiment score, the change to the previous sentiment score is the basis for the correlation analysis. It is expected to deliver similar, but possibly more unambiguous results.

Pearson Product Moment Correlation – BMW and Audi		
Statistic	Variable X (BMW)	Variable Y (Audi)
Mean	-0.014760147601476	0
Biased Variance	106.900151141733	123.926199261993
Biased Standard Deviation	10.3392529295754	11.1322144814944
Covariance	-3.63333333333333	
Correlation	**-0.0314506040969467**	
Determination	0.000989140498062878	
T-Test	-0.516083562883647	
p-value (2 sided)	0.606219992220046	
p-value (1 sided)	0.303109996110023	
Kendall tau Rank Correlation		
Kendall tau	-0.0187808685004711	
2-sided p-value	0.657646954059601	
Score	-660	
Var(Score)	2211268.5	
Denominator	35142.14453125	

Table 25 – Relative Sentiment Score – Correlation between BMW and Audi

Pearson Product Moment Correlation – BMW and Mercedes

Statistic	Variable X (BMW)	Variable Y (Mercedes)
Mean	-0.014760147601476	-0.00738007380073801
Biased Variance	106.900151141733	55.7342628776841
Biased Standard Deviation	10.3392529295754	7.46553835149778
Covariance	1.76655733223999	
Correlation	**0.0228019463508786**	
Determination	0.000519928757388344	
T-Test	0.37407698570705	
p-value (2 sided)	0.70864172366226	
p-value (1 sided)	0.35432086183113	
Kendall tau Rank Correlation		
Kendall tau	0.0784549787640572	
2-sided p-value	0.0666632652282715	
Score	2724	
Var(Score)	2204581.75	
Denominator	34720.55078125	

Table 26 – Relative Sentiment Score – Correlation between BMW and Mercedes

Pearson Product Moment Correlation – Mercedes and Audi

Statistic	Variable X (Mercedes)	Variable Y (Audi)
Mean	-0.00738007380073801	0
Biased Variance	55.7342628776841	123.926199261993
Biased Standard Deviation	7.46553835149778	11.1322144814944
Covariance	-11.337037037037	
Correlation	**-0.135909978166721**	
Determination	0.0184715221652785	
T-Test	-2.24996638854816	
p-value (2 sided)	0.0252595399345556	
p-value (1 sided)	0.0126297699672778	
Kendall tau Rank Correlation		
Kendall tau	-0.0929827988147736	
2-sided p-value	0.0287557151168585	
Score	-3251	
Var(Score)	2208721.25	
Denominator	34963.45703125	

Table 27 – Relative Sentiment Score – Correlation between Mercedes and Audi

The results are thoroughly comparable to the absolute sentiment scores. The correlations are a little higher (especially between Mercedes and Audi with correlation values approximately -0.1), but still in a negligible area.

Computer Operating System Market

The next section will apply the same principle to the market of computer operating systems.

Pearson Product Moment Correlation – Windows and Linux		
Statistic	Variable X (Windows)	Variable Y (Linux)
Mean	-0.014760147601476	-0.0479704797047971
Biased Variance	29.5569777099985	37.0050789068776
Biased Standard Deviation	5.43663293868535	6.0831799995461
Covariance	3.48077080770808	
Correlation	**0.104859847538663**	
Determination	0.0109955876258317	
T-Test	1.72936333611634	
p-value (2 sided)	0.0848912691277026	
p-value (1 sided)	0.0424456345638513	
Kendall tau Rank Correlation		
Kendall tau	0.0582531243562698	
2-sided p-value	0.189963579177856	
Score	1931	
Var(Score)	2168287	
Denominator	33148.4375	

Table 28 – Relative Sentiment Score – Correlation between Windows and Linux

Pearson Product Moment Correlation – Windows and Mac OS X

Statistic	Variable X (Windows)	Variable Y (Mac OS X)
Mean	-0.014760147601476	0.022140221402214
Biased Variance	29.5569777099985	103.490284718345
Biased Standard Deviation	5.43663293868535	10.1730174834385
Covariance	-2.64411644116441	
Correlation	**-0.0476316084214236**	
Determination	0.00226877012081183	
T-Test	-0.782104174359225	
p-value (2 sided)	0.434841233883592	
p-value (1 sided)	0.217420616941796	
Kendall tau Rank Correlation		
Kendall tau	-0.0714087635278702	
2-sided p-value	0.102646745741367	
Score	-2412	
Var(Score)	2182083.75	
Denominator	33777.3671875	

Table 29 – Relative Sentiment Score – Correlation between Windows and Mac OS X

Pearson Product Moment Correlation – Linux and Mac OS X

Statistic	Variable X (Linux)	Variable Y (Mac OS X)
Mean	-0.0479704797047971	0.022140221402214
Biased Variance	37.0050789068776	103.490284718345
Biased Standard Deviation	6.0831799995461	10.1730174834385
Covariance	7.12328823288233	
Correlation	**0.114681808454671**	
Determination	0.0131519171904339	
T-Test	1.89341372971984	
p-value (2 sided)	0.0593759498092123	
p-value (1 sided)	0.0296879749046062	
Kendall tau Rank Correlation		
Kendall tau	0.0497224815189838	
2-sided p-value	0.252918481826782	
Score	1693	
Var(Score)	2190223.75	
Denominator	34048.984375	

Table 30 – Relative Sentiment Score – Correlation between Linux and Mac OS X

Analogous to the premium car market, the correlation values increased, but are not significant. The correlations are still weak and inconsistent in regards to the orientation. Again, Linux holds a positive sentiment correlation with both competitors, even though they are vastly different in feature emphasizes and ideologies. Before coming to a conclusion, the next section will compute the correlations between smartphone market competitors.

Smartphone Operating Systems Market

The absolute sentiment score correlations in the smartphone market were low towards Windows Phone. Only between Android and iOS was there a noticeable correlation. The next few tables list the statistical values of the correlation of the changes of the sentiment score.

Pearson Product Moment Correlation – Android and Windows Phone		
Statistic	Variable X (Android)	Variable Y (Windows Phone)
Mean	-0.029520295202952	-0.022140221402214
Biased Variance	20.8256968178538	57.4902847183453
Biased Standard Deviation	4.5635180308457	7.58223481028815
Covariance	1.20675140084734	
Correlation	**0.0347468375940076**	
Determination	0.00120734272278434	
T-Test	0.570234847570302	
p-value (2 sided)	0.568994388888726	
p-value (1 sided)	0.284497194444363	
Kendall tau Rank Correlation		
Kendall tau	0.0316995643079281	
2-sided p-value	0.471141815185547	
Score	1065	
Var(Score)	2180055.75	
Denominator	33596.67578125	

Table 31 – Relative Sentiment Score – Correlation between Android and Windows Phone

Pearson Product Moment Correlation – iOS and Windows Phone

Statistic	Variable X (iOS)	Variable Y (Windows Phone)
Mean	-0.0738007380073801	-0.022140221402214
Biased Variance	54.9761032665677	57.4902847183453
Biased Standard Deviation	7.41458719461628	7.58223481028815
Covariance	-2.24978816454831	
Correlation	**-0.03987051950834**	
Determination	0.00158965832586492	
T-Test	-0.654445519987278	
p-value (2 sided)	0.513383960405477	
p-value (1 sided)	0.256691980202739	
Kendall tau Rank Correlation		
Kendall tau	-0.0208475887775421	
2-sided p-value	0.632753968238831	
Score	-708	
Var(Score)	2189011.75	
Denominator	33960.76171875	

Table 32 – Relative Sentiment Score – Correlation between iOS and Windows Phone

Pearson Product Moment Correlation – Android and iOS

Statistic	Variable X (Android)	Variable Y (iOS)
Mean	-0.029520295202952	-0.0738007380073801
Biased Variance	20.8256968178538	54.9761032665677
Biased Standard Deviation	4.5635180308457	7.41458719461628
Covariance	24.9274429410961	
Correlation	**0.733982079437194**	
Determination	0.538729692934948	
T-Test	17.7249021760121	
p-value (2 sided)	0	
p-value (1 sided)	0	
Kendall tau Rank Correlation		
Kendall tau	0.303675621747971	
2-sided p-value	0	
Score	10086	
Var(Score)	2169666.25	
Denominator	33213.0703125	

Table 33 – Relative Sentiment Score – Correlation between Android and iOS

Once again, the correlation values were very similar to the previous test of absolute sentiment scores. The correlation between iOS and Android continues to stand out. The correlation values are now even higher (0.73 and 0.3 as Pearson and Kendall correlation, respectively).

To conclude, there are two key takeaways from the data of the first two hypotheses. First, in the general marketplace, the correlation of sentiments is unexpectedly low. Second, the sentiment does exist when moving to very emotional products and a young market. However, it was surprising that the two main rivals, iOS and Android, are *positively* correlated. Common sense dictates that there might be an error. In order to cross-check the phenomenon, that rivals in a very emotional domain might be positively correlated, the data for two sports rivals was additionally examined. Two football clubs were chosen, Chelsea F.C. and Arsenal, which is one of the top rivalries in English-speaking sports [91].

Pearson Product Moment Correlation – Arsenal and Chelsea F.C.		
Statistic	Variable X (Arsenal)	Variable Y (Chelsea F.C)
Mean	-0.0922509225092251	-0.025830258302583
Biased Variance	58.7922277746763	50.268705491483
Biased Standard Deviation	7.66760899985623	7.09004270025809
Covariance	10.0568675686757	
Correlation	**0.184309786196218**	
Determination	0.0339700972876958	
T-Test	3.07559573787666	
p-value (2 sided)	0.00231725409778516	
p-value (1 sided)	0.00115862704889258	
Kendall tau Rank Correlation		
Kendall tau	0.124747425317764	
2-sided p-value	0.00327026844024658	
Score	4375	
Var(Score)	2211726.25	
Denominator	35070.86328125	

Table 34 – Relative Sentiment Score – Correlation between Arsenal and Chelsea F.C.

It can be fairly certain, that the sentiments of the fan bases of these two teams are strongly negatively correlated. Yet, similar to the iOS-Android phenomenon, a positive correlation is observed as well (see Table 34). The data verifies the iOS-Android tendency, even though the correlation is weaker. Nevertheless, the two sentiments are *positively* correlated too.

One possible explanation could be that both terms are mentioned in the same tweet and the sentiment accounts for both, e.g.

"Android is so much better than iOS."

The "better" indicates a positive sentiment. However, since the analysis system does not include a comparison detection algorithm yet, the tweet will count a positive sentiment for both keywords. This might explain the positive correlation. Yet, checking the data, less than 5% of all tweets contained both keywords. Since the number is too low to influence the overall result, this cannot be the explanation for the positive sentiment.

One aspect not discussed so far, which could explain the unexpected positive correlations, might be the longevity of the collected data. The time span covers a full nine months. However, often there are noticeable changes of the sentiment when there is a significant *event* for the company or product. This could be a highly publicized bug or error of the product; it might be a presentation of a new (competitor) product; or any other potent stimulus of the sentiment. The next hypothesis is built upon the thought that these market-influencing events cause an abnormal high tweet count.

5.2.3. Third Hypothesis

- H3: The sentiment towards Company A moves, when company B's sentiment goes up or down, while only considering the top 25 events (equals top 10%), An event is defined as the largest amount of tweets sent per time unit (in this case: days).

The third hypothesis will examine the previously recognized correlation of relative sentiment score changes between Android and iOS—however, only the top 25 days will be considered, which are based upon the overall number of tweets sent. This leads to the following table:

Pearson Product Moment Correlation – Android and iOS (Top 25)		
Statistic	Variable X (Android)	Variable Y (iOS)
Mean	-0.24	-0.56
Biased Variance	47.7024	304.6464
Biased Standard Deviation	6.90669240664444	17.4541227221536
Covariance	113.735	
Correlation	**0.90572681332385**	
Determination	0.820341060373775	
T-Test	10.2479436061291	
p-value (2 sided)	4.80607109665243e-10	
p-value (1 sided)	2.40303554832622e-10	
Degrees of Freedom	23	
Number of Observations	25	
Kendall tau Rank Correlation		
Kendall tau	0.660974383354187	
2-sided p-value	6.55651092529297e-06	
Score	193	
Var(Score)	1815.53393554688	
Denominator	291.9931640625	

Table 35 – Correlation between Android and iOS (Top 25 Events)

A correlation already existed between Android and iOS, even when considering the data of the full nine months. The correlation of the relative sentiment score changes, limited to the top 25 events, is even stronger with a positive Pearson coefficient of approximately 0.91. Thus, the correlation between these two competitors is more evident when only considering *events*. The next three tables test the same hypothesis that the correlation values increase when only considering the top 25 events, in the premium car market.

Pearson Product Moment Correlation – Audi and BMW (Top 25)

Statistic	Variable X (Audi)	Variable Y (BMW)
Mean	-3.92	4.96
Biased Variance	88.6336	132.1984
Biased Standard Deviation	9.41454194318555	11.4977563028619
Covariance	3.045	
Correlation	**0.0270051277401856**	
Determination	0.000729276924263743	
T-Test	0.129559293825447	
p-value (2 sided)	0.898041491639048	
p-value (1 sided)	0.449020745819524	
Kendall tau Rank Correlation		
Kendall tau	0.0105456141754985	
2-sided p-value	0.96225905418396	
Score	3	
Var(Score)	1786.45556640625	
Denominator	284.478454589844	

Table 36 – Correlation between Audi and BMW (Top 25 Events)

Pearson Product Moment Correlation – Audi and Mercedes (Top 25)

Statistic	Variable X	Variable Y
Mean	-3.92	-0.6
Biased Variance	88.6336	84.32
Biased Standard Deviation	9.41454194318555	9.1825922265992
Covariance	-29.95	
Correlation	**-0.332585695432691**	
Determination	0.110613244806447	
T-Test	-1.69130586700932	
p-value (2 sided)	0.104286096874002	
p-value (1 sided)	0.0521430484370012	
Kendall tau Rank Correlation		
Kendall tau	-0.230408981442451	
2-sided p-value	0.12475473433733	
Score	-66	
Var(Score)	1792.84582519531	
Denominator	286.447174072266	

Table 37 – Correlation between Audi and Mercedes (Top 25 Events)

Pearson Product Moment Correlation – BMW and Mercedes		
Statistic	Variable X (BMW)	Variable Y (Mercedes)
Mean	4.96	-0.6
Biased Variance	132.1984	84.32
Biased Standard Deviation	11.4977563028619	9.1825922265992
Covariance	25.4333333333333	
Correlation	**0.231257655209368**	
Determination	0.053480103092935	
T-Test	1.13997456634258	
p-value (2 sided)	0.26602977625288	
p-value (1 sided)	0.13301488812644	
Degrees of Freedom	23	
Number of Observations	25	
Kendall tau Rank Correlation		
Kendall tau	0.117244176566601	
2-sided p-value	0.437902688980103	
Score	34	
Var(Score)	1809.65478515625	
Denominator	289.993072509766	

Table 38 – Correlation between BMW and Mercedes (Top 25 Events)

The correlation values are interesting. There is still no correlation between the two competitors Audi and BMW (less than 0.03 for each correlation coefficient), even though both have a very similar brand and offer comparable products. However, Audi and Mercedes have a stronger negative correlation than prior results. Previously, the Pearson correlation was -0.13. When only considering the top 25 events, the negative correlation grows to a Pearson coefficient of -0.33. Lastly, BMW and Mercedes had no correlation previously (Pearson coefficient of 0.02), however, a correlation of 0.23 was found when studying only the top 25 events.

In conclusion, the direction of significant correlations stayed the same under the premise of reducing the dataset to the 25 most significant days and thus, reducing possible noise. The strength of the correlation grew considerably for three out of four correlated competitors.

The third hypothesis cannot be fully supported, because there are still competitors (e.g. BMW and Audi) whose sentiment scores do not seem to be correlated at all. On the other hand, the sentiment between Android and iOS grew throughout each analysis and is still positive. The most reasonable explanation is that a positive tweet about Company A causes the fans of Company B to respond with a positive sentiment as well. Consequently, both sentiments increase and are positively correlated. Nevertheless, in order to examine this hypothesis, tweets must be collected as a conversation graph instead of a list. The current system design is not yet capable of completing this task. Ritter et al. [92] showed that it is possible to model Twitter conversations as a graph. This should be the next step to further investigate the positivity of competitor correlations.

	Market Form	Market Maturity
Low Sentiment Correlation	Oligopoly	Stage 3 and Stage 4 (mature)
Medium Sentiment Correlation	Monopoly	
High Sentiment Correlation	Duopoly (between them)	Stage 1 and 2 (immature)

Table 39 – Indications for Correlation Strengths based on Market Types

To conclude this chapter, the collected data of millions of tweets over nine months in various markets is a very interesting base for further research. This means another one of the goals of the thesis was met. Nevertheless, not all correlation results were as expected. Although more analysis must be completed in the future, these preliminary results suggest that the correlations between competitors are dependent on the market form and the market maturity. Table 39 recapitulates the indication the analyses in this chapter extracted from the data. This thesis will be concluded with the next chapter.

6. Conclusion

This master thesis has pushed the boundaries of research in several areas. Firstly, it designed and implemented a scalable and rapid sentiment analysis system for data from social networks. The cluster of servers pulls data from Twitter's streaming APIs, but can be used for any structured data source. The system can calculate the sentiment of thousands of tweets in a short time and give a near-real-time estimation of the average sentiment. It additionally runs further algorithms to increase the sentiment scoring precision. The results are provided in several databases, which are designed for different aspects. These databases are used to showcase the capabilities of the system.

Secondly, the system is used to exhibit several commercial use cases. Businesses could gain a substantial competitive advantage by attaining more information about their customers, the company's products, competitors, and the entire market. Furthermore, the method is low-cost and, unlike other methods, non-intrusive. Instead of marketing departments attempting to draw conclusions from small research groups or surveys, the system taps into the unfiltered stream of their customers' opinions.

Thirdly, the direct access opens an entirely new approach to view marketplaces from a business research perspective. This master thesis proved the use of the system in multiple markets. The sentiment scores were used to examine the relations between competitors in different market types. The results were partially as expected, but also somewhat surprising. An expected result was that the sentiments of competitors do not correlate when they are competing in a market of a matured and unemotional product, e.g. premium cars. The data also supported that the correlation strength changes when the product carries more emotion. For example, the smartphone market is a very young market and, out of the researched markets, had the highest correlations. An unforeseen outcome was that the key competitors in a duopoly had positively correlated sentiments. This thesis delivers possible causes for the unanticipated positivity of the correlation.

Lastly, the system has significantly more possible use cases than demonstrated. This is only the tip of the iceberg. For example, the scalable sentiment analysis system was not used for social science purposes. If extended, the system could also track and analyze entire conversations. The system could use this feature's additional information to gain more knowledge about products, and the behavior of customers and businesses in a marketplace. To conclude, having a structured model of conversations opens a new opportunity for social sciences. While the thesis was focused on business and economic topics, the system could also be used for social research [83].

6.1. Limitations of Findings and Further Work

The design of the scalable sentiment analysis system is complex, even though many decisions were made to simplify the architecture. The system consumed data only from Twitter, due to the design of their API and easiness of access to the data. Twitter also delivered interesting supplementary information, like geolocation, for an extra perspective into the data. Nevertheless, using just one data source severely limits the system. For one, it is dependent upon Twitter. If Twitter or their APIs shut down, the system renders useless. Also, the data is distorted towards the demographics of Twitter. While Twitter is one of the more balanced social networks and attracts around 19% of Internet users [93], it lately trends towards young men [94]. Generally, Twitter overly represents the young and well-educated participants of our society. Consequently, this misrepresentation can twist the overall insights and results of the system. This can affect commercial and scientific use cases. Future work should focus on adding one or more sources from other social networks to the system. Technically, this should not be a challenge. However, it is not the only possible technical improvement.

As with any computer system, it can be further optimized and improved. While the work in this thesis showed that MapReduce algorithms are capable of providing near-real-time sentiment results, it still has a larger time delay than necessary. MapReduce has several successors, which have improved the capabilities to work on stream data and directly provide real-time results. One option would be to stay within the Hadoop ecosystem, but switch to the Apache Spark [95] as a processing engine.

Furthermore, the system cannot just be faster; it also can be more precise. Although a basic sentiment-scoring algorithm with pre- and post-processing was implemented with state-of-the-art parts, using additional algorithms and further tuning the existing ones can increase its accuracy. For example, the part-of-speech tagging can be customized for the different language patterns of each social network [96]. Moreover, the current algorithm is fixed and does not automatically improve. There has been research for interactive learning phases during sentiment scoring for better results [97]. Sentiment analysis is a very young, ongoing research field, which continuous to improve constantly. Keeping up to date for more precise sentiment scores can benefit the usage possibilities.

Currently, this may not be the largest limitation. The geographical tool presented in an earlier section is powerful, but is restricted due to the language limitations of the system. If a country has two different languages, a multilingual system is required. Currently, it is limited to one customer base which is speaking the same language. The scoring algorithm should be adjusted to handle multiple languages, as Denecke [33] outlined. Parts of the SentiWordNet database already exist for the Spanish [98] and German languages [99], [100]. In conclusion, implementing further languages significantly widens the scope of the system.

Correspondingly, the geographical tool also disregards one aspect: variances in language terms and interpretation depending on the location. One example would be the term pizza. While pizza likely generates a lot of positive sentiment around the world, the preferred style of eaten pizzas is vastly diverse. The system is imperfect as the semantic of words is not distinguishable. To a degree, the product features analysis presented earlier can assist in diminishing the effect of this phenomenon. Using the product feature sentiment extraction, companies can understand why a pizza is especially liked in various regions.

Similarly, the scientific analysis of different markets was limited to English-speaking users. Since it is essentially based on the emotions of customers to the products of the market, it might result in an altered outcome on another customer base. Germans, for example, invest more in their cars than other nations. Therefore, the scientific analysis presented in the previous chapter might change, if it extracts tweets from German-speaking users.

Overall, the system has numerous limitations. It is technically not matured yet and still requires improvements for faster and more accurate results. The data representation in the databases requires more optimization to support more scalable usage scenarios. Additionally, due to the limitation to Twitter as platform, it was restricted to one source. Furthermore, the sentiment-scoring algorithm is only implemented for the English language.

Lastly, the concept of narrowing down sentiments to a positive/negative scale and possibly an emotional/factual scale is an oversimplification of human emotions. While the research of sentiment analysis is not yet at the point of further understanding the many dimensions of moods and feelings, other parts of the system can be improved. The technical improvements were already outlined. The extension to numerous sources and the support for multiple languages was already explained as well. At this point, the system just needs more work to develop into a more complete structure.

However, already in this very early stage, the shown cases demonstrated how powerful the system can be. Analyzing users' sentiment in social networks gives a whole new approach to understand economic markets. This has large potential for business, economic, and social scientific interests. If the system can already achieve these results in such an early stage, its potential is immense when further enhanced.

7. Bibliography

[1]   B. Liu, Sentiment Analysis and Opinion Mining (Synthesis Lectures on Human Language Technologies), Morgan & Claypool Publishers, 2012.

[2]   B. Pang, L. Lee and S. Vaithyanathan, "Thumbs up?: sentiment classification using machine learning techniques," in *ACL-02 conference on Empirical methods in natural language processing*, 2002.

[3]   P. D. Turney , "Thumbs up or thumbs down?: semantic orientation applied to unsupervised classification of reviews," in *Proceedings of the 40th Annual Meeting on Association for Computational Linguistics*, Philadelphia, Pennsylvania, 2002.

[4]   M. Taboada, J. Brooke, M. Tofiloski, K. Voll and M. Stede, "Lexicon-based methods for sentiment analysis," *Computational Linguistics,* vol. 2, no. 267-307, p. 37, 2011.

[5]   B. Pang and L. Lee, "A sentimental education: sentiment analysis using subjectivity summarization based on minimum cuts," in *Proceedings of the 42nd Annual Meeting on Association for Computational Linguistics*, Barcelona, Spain, 2004.

[6]   C. Whitelaw, N. Garg and S. Argamon , "Using appraisal groups for sentiment analysis," in *14th ACM international conference on Information and knowledge management*, Bremen, Germany, 2005.

[7]   H. Shi, G. Zhou and P. Qian, "An Attribute-based Sentiment Analysis System," *Information Technology Journal,* vol. 9, pp. 1607-1614, 2010.

[8]   W. Kessler and J. Kuhn, "A Corpus of Comparisons in Product Reviews," in *International Conference on Language Resources and Evaluation,*

Reykjavik, Iceland, 2014.

[9]   T. Nasukawa and J. Yi, "Sentiment analysis: capturing favorability using natural language processing," in *Proceedings of the 2nd international conference on Knowledge capture*, Sanibel Island, FL, USA, 2003.

[10]   P. Kherwa, A. Sachdeva, D. Mahajan, N. Pande and P. K. Singh, "An approach towards comprehensive sentimental data analysis and opinion mining," in *IEEE International Advance Computing Conference (IACC)*, Gurgaon, 2014.

[11]   W. Kasper and M. Vela, "Sentiment Analysis for Hotel Reviews," in *Computational Linguistics-Applications Conference*, 2011.

[12]   A. Kennedy and D. Inkpen, "Sentiment classification of movie reviews using contextual valence shifters," in *Computational Intelligence*, 2006.

[13]   T. Mullen and R. Malouf, "A Preliminary Investigation into Sentiment Analysis of Informal Political Discourse," in *AAAI Spring Symposium: Computational Approaches to Analyzing Weblogs*, 2006.

[14]   A.-M. Popescu and O. Etzioni, "Extracting Product Features and Opinions from Reviews," in *Natural language processing and text mining*, London, Springer, 2007, pp. 9-28.

[15]   T. Weninger, X. A. Zhu and J. Han, "An exploration of discussion threads in social news sites: a case study of the Reddit community," in *IEEE/ACM International Conference on Advances in Social Networks Analysis and Mining*, Niagara, Ontario, Canada, 2013.

[16]   N. Godbole, M. Srinivasaiah and S. Skiena, "Large-Scale Sentiment Analysis for News and Blogs," in *ICWSM 7*, 2007.

[17]   S. Thanangthanakij, E. Pacharawongsakda, N. Tongtep, P. Aimmanee and T. Theeramunkong, "An Empirical Study on Multi-dimensional Sentiment Analysis from User Service Reviews," in *Seventh International Conference*

on *Knowledge, Information and Creativity Support Systems (KICSS),* Melbourne, VIC, 2012.

[18]   L. Zhuang, F. Jing and X.-Y. Zhu, "Movie review mining and summarization," in *15th ACM international conference on Information and knowledge management*, Arlington, Virginia, USA, 2006.

[19]   M. Hu and B. Liu , "Mining and summarizing customer reviews," in *10th ACM SIGKDD international conference on Knowledge discovery and data mining*, Seattle, WA, USA, 2004.

[20]   N. Jindal and B. Liu, "Opinion spam and analysis," *Proceedings of the 2008 International Conference on Web Search and Data Mining, ACM,* pp. 219-230, 2008.

[21]   A. Tumasjan, T. O. Sprenger, P. G. Sandner and I. M. Welpe, "Predicting Elections with Twitter: What 140 Characters Reveal about Political Sentiment.," *ICWSM,* vol. 10, pp. 178-185, 2010.

[22]   B. A. Huberman and S. Asur, "Predicting the Future with Social Media," in *IEEE/WIC/ACM International Conference on Web Intelligence and Intelligent Agent Technology (WI-IAT)*, Toronto, ON, Canada, 2010.

[23]   J. Bollen, H. Mao and X. Zeng, "Twitter mood predicts the stock market," *Journal of Computational Science,* vol. 2, no. 1, pp. 1-8, 2011.

[24]   A. C. Madrigal, "The Atlantic," 18 March 2011. [Online]. Available: http://www.theatlantic.com/technology/archive/2011/03/does-anne-hathaway-news-drive-berkshire-hathaways-stock/72661/. [Accessed 06 June 2014].

[25]   A. Celikyilmaz, D. Hakkani-Tur and J. Feng, "Probabilistic model-based sentiment analysis of twitter messages," *Spoken Language Technology Workshop (SLT), IEEE,* pp. 79 - 84, 2010.

[26]   B. Pang and L. Lee, "Opinion Mining and Sentiment Analysis," *Foundations and Trends in Information Retrieval,* vol. 2, no. 1-2, pp. 1-135, 2008.

[27]   Y. Choi and C. Cardie, "Learning with Compositional Semantics as Structural Inference for Subsentential Sentiment Analysis," in *Proceedings of the Conference on Empirical Methods in Natural Language Processing,* Honolulu, Hawaii, 2008.

[28]   I. G. Councill, R. McDonald and L. Velikovich, "What's great and what's not: learning to classify the scope of negation for improved sentiment analysis," in *Proceedings of the Workshop on Negation and Speculation in Natural Language Processing,* Uppsala, Sweden, 2010.

[29]   L. Jia, C. Yu and W. Meng, "The Effect of Negation on Sentiment Analysis and Retrieval Effectiveness," in *Proceedings of the 18th ACM conference on Information and knowledge management,* Hong Kong, China, 2009.

[30]   P. Carvalho, L. Sarmento, M. J. Silva and E. de Oliveira, "Clues for detecting irony in user-generated contents: oh...!! it's "so easy" ;-)," in *Proceedings of the 1st international CIKM workshop on Topic-sentiment analysis for mass opinion,* Hong Kong, China, 2009.

[31]   M. Wiegand, A. Balahur, B. Roth, D. Klakow and A. Montoyo, "A survey on the role of negation in sentiment analysis," in *Proceedings of the Workshop on Negation and Speculation in Natural Language Processing,* Uppsala, Sweden, 2010.

[32]   J. Zhang and S. Tan, "An empirical study of sentiment analysis for chinese documents," *Expert Systems with Applications,* vol. 34, no. 4, pp. 2622-2629, 2008.

[33]   K. Denecke, "Using SentiWordNet for multilingual sentiment analysis," in *IEEE 24th International Conference on Data Engineering Workshop,* Cancun, 2008.

[34]   K. Hiroshi, N. Tetsuya and W. Hideo, "Deeper sentiment analysis using machine translation technology," in *Proceedings of the 20th international conference on Computational Linguistics*, 2004.

[35]   M. Bautin, L. Vijayarenu and S. Skie, "International Sentiment Analysis for News and Blogs," in *ICWSM*, 2008.

[36]   J. Boyd-Graber and P. Resnik , "Holistic sentiment analysis across languages: multilingual supervised latent Dirichlet allocation," in *Proceedings of the 2010 Conference on Empirical Methods in Natural Language Processing*, Cambridge, Massachusetts, 2010.

[37]   A. Abbasi, H. Chen and A. Salem , "Sentiment analysis in multiple languages: Feature selection for opinion classification in Web forums," *ACM Trans. Inf. Syst.,* vol. 26, no. 3, pp. 1-34, 2008.

[38]   J. B. Walther and K. P. D'Addario, "The impacts of emoticons on message interpretation in computer-mediated communication," *Social science computer review,* vol. 19, no. 3, pp. 324-347, 2001.

[39]   J. Read , "Using emoticons to reduce dependency in machine learning techniques for sentiment classification," in *Proceedings of the ACL Student Research Workshop*, Ann Arbor, Michigan, 2005.

[40]   A. Aue and M. Gamon, "Customizing Sentiment Classifiers to New Domains: a Case Study," in *Proceedings of recent advances in natural language processing (RANLP)*, 2005.

[41]   A. Fahrni and M. Klenner, "Old wine or warm beer: Target-specific sentiment analysis of adjectives," in *Proc. of the Symposium on Affective Language in Human and Machine, AISB*, 2008.

[42]   F. Benamara, C. Cesarano, A. Picariello, D. Reforgiato and V. Subrahmanian, "Sentiment Analysis: Adjectives and Adverbs are better than Adjectives Alone," in *ICWSM*, 2007.

[43]   M. S. Usha and M. Indra Devi, "Analysis of Sentiments using Unsupervised Learning Techniques," in *International Conference on Information Communication and Embedded Systems (ICICES)*, Chennai, India, 2013.

[44]   S. Tan, G. Wu, H. Tang and X. Cheng, "A Novel Scheme for Domain-transfer Problem in the context of Sentiment Analysis," in *Proceedings of the sixteenth ACM conference on Conference on information and knowledge management* , Lisbon, Portugal, 2007.

[45]   C. J. Van Rijsbergen, Information Retrieval, 2nd ed., Newton, MA, USA: Butterworth-Heinemann, 1979.

[46]   D. M. Powers, "Evaluation: from precision, recall and F-measure to ROC, informedness, markedness and correlation," *Bioinfo Publications, 2011.*

[47]   N. Mehra, S. Khandelwal and P. Patel , "Sentiment Identification Using Maximum Entropy Analysis of Movie Reviews," 2002.

[48]   F. Batista and R. Ribeiro, "Sentiment Analysis and Topic Classification based on Binary Maximum Entropy Classifiers," *Procesamiento del Lenguaje Natural,* pp. 77-84, 2013.

[49]   S. Baccianella, A. Esuli and F. Sebastiani, "SentiWordNet 3.0: An Enhanced Lexical Resource for Sentiment Analysis and Opinion Mining," in *LREC*, 2010.

[50]   H. Ameur and S. Jamoussi, "Dynamic construction of dictionaries for sentiment classification," in *IEEE 13th International Conference on Data Mining Workshops*, Dallas, TX , 2013.

[51]   H. Kanayama and T. Nasukawa, "Fully automatic lexicon expansion for domain-oriented sentiment analysis," in *Proceedings of the 2006 Conference on Empirical Methods in Natural Language Processing*, 2006.

[52]   R. Batool, A. M. Khattak, J. Maqbool and S. Lee, "Precise tweet classification and sentiment analysis," in *IEEE/ACIS 12th International*

Conference on Computer and Information Science (ICIS), Niigata, 2013.

[53]   A. Andreevskaia and S. Bergler, "ClaC and ClaC-NB: knowledge-based and corpus-based approaches to sentiment tagging," in *Proceedings of the 4th International Workshop on Semantic Evaluations*, Prague, Czech Republic, 2007.

[54]   R. Prabowo and M. Thelwall, "Sentiment Analysis: A Combined Approach," *Journal of Informetrics*, vol. 3, no. 2, pp. 143-157, 2009.

[55]   A. Agarwal, B. Xie, I. Vovsha, O. Rambow and R. Passonneau , "Sentiment analysis of Twitter data," in *Proceedings of the Workshop on Languages in Social Media*, Portland, Oregon, 2011.

[56]   B. J. Jansen, M. Zhang, K. Sobel and A. Chowdury, "Micro-blogging as online word of mouth branding," in *CHI '09 Extended Abstracts on Human Factors in Computing Systems*, Boston, MA, USA, 2009.

[57]   C. Tan, L. Lee, J. Tang, L. Jiang, M. Zhou and P. Li, "User-Level Sentiment Analysis Incorporating Social Networks," in *Proceedings of the 17th ACM SIGKDD international conference on Knowledge discovery and data mining*, San Diego, California, USA, 2011.

[58]   M. Thelwall, K. Buckley and G. Paltoglou, "Sentiment strength detection for the social web," *Journal of the American Society for Information Science and Technology*, vol. 63, no. 1, pp. 163-173, 2012.

[59]   A. Pak and P. Paroubek, "Twitter as a Corpus for Sentiment Analysis and Opinion Mining," in *LREC*, 2010.

[60]   M. A. Beyer and D. Laney, "The importance of'big data': a definition," *Stamford, CT: Gartner,* 2012.

[61]   S. Lohr, "The age of big data," *New York Times,* vol. 11, 2012.

[62]   A. McAfee, E. Brynjolfsson, T. H. Davenport, D. Patil and D. Barton, "Big

Data," *The management revolution. Harvard Bus Rev,* vol. 90, no. 10, pp. 61-67, 2012.

[63] Twitter Inc., "REST APIs | Twitter Developers:," 2014. [Online]. Available: https://dev.twitter.com/rest/public. [Accessed 15 10 2014].

[64] reddit inc., "reddit.com: api documentation," 2014. [Online]. Available: http://www.reddit.com/dev/api. [Accessed 05 10 2014].

[65] Twitter Inc., "About Twitter, Inc. | About," 2014. [Online]. Available: https://about.twitter.com/company. [Accessed 05 10 2014].

[66] Twitter Inc., "The Streaming APIs," 2014. [Online]. Available: https://dev.twitter.com/streaming/overview. [Accessed 03 10 2014].

[67] S. Haberman, "Euro 2012 Goal Smashes Tweets-Per-Second Sports Record," Mashable, 02 July 2012. [Online]. Available: http://mashable.com/2012/07/02/euro-2012-tweet-record/. [Accessed 13 June 2014].

[68] IBM Inc., "What Is Watson?," IBM, [Online]. Available: http://www.ibm.com/smarterplanet/us/en/ibmwatson/. [Accessed 13 June 2014].

[69] SAP, "What is SAP Hana?," [Online]. Available: http://www.saphana.com/community/about-hana. [Accessed 13 June 2014].

[70] A. Thusoo, J. S. Sarma, N. Jain, Z. Shao, P. Chakka, N. Zhang, S. Antony, H. Liu and R. Murthy, "Hive-a petabyte scale data warehouse using hadoop," in *IEEE 26th International Conference on Data Engineering (ICDE),* 2010.

[71] L. George, HBase: the definitive guide, O'Reilly Media, Inc., 2011.

[72] J. Dean and S. Ghemawat, "MapReduce: simplified data processing on large clusters," *Communications of the ACM,* vol. 51, no. 1, pp. 107-113, 2008.

[73]   B. Liu, E. Blasch, Y. Chen, S. Dan and G. Chen, "Scalable Sentiment Classification for Big Data Analysis Using Naïve Bayes Classifier," in *IEEE International Conference on Big Data*, Silicon Valley, CA, USA, 2013.

[74]   M. P. Marcus, M. A. Marcinkiewicz and B. Santorini, "Building a large annotated corpus of English: The Penn Treebank," *Computational linguistics,* vol. 19, no. 2, pp. 313-330, 1993.

[75]   The Apache Software Foundation, "Apache OpenNLP," 2010. [Online]. Available: https://opennlp.apache.org/. [Accessed 12 08 2014].

[76]   Cloudera, Inc., "Cloudera QuickStart VM," 2014. [Online]. Available: http://www.cloudera.com/content/cloudera/en/documentation/DemoVMs/Cl oudera-QuickStart-VM/cloudera_quickstart_vm.html. [Accessed   04   09 2014].

[77]   E. F. Codd, S. B. Codd and C. Salley, "Providing OLAP (on-line analytical processing) to user-analysts: An IT mandate," *Codd and Date,* vol. 32, 1993.

[78]   J. Horrigan, "Online Shopping," Pew Research Internet Project, 2008.

[79]   N. Dixon, B. Jakic and R. Lagerweij, "FoodMood: Measuring global food sentiment one tweet at a time," Sixth International AAAI Conference on Weblogs and Social Media, Dublin, Ireland, 2012.

[80]   Highcharts, "What is Highcharts?," 2014. [Online]. Available: http://www.highcharts.com/products/highcharts. [Accessed 27 09 2014].

[81]   Merriam-Webster, "Market," [Online]. Available: http://www.merriam-webster.com. [Accessed 07 10 2014].

[82]   R. H. Frank and B. Bernanke, Principles of Microeconomics, McGraw-Hill/Irwin, 2010.

[83]   R. B. McKenzie and G. Tullock, "In Defense of Monopoly," in *The New*

World of Economics, Springer, 2012, pp. 383-390.

[84]   M. Courtney, "Upwardly mobile [Communications Enterprise Mobile]," *Engineering & Technology*, vol. 8, no. 7, 2013.

[85]   E. González, C. Ana and V. Juan, "How car dealers adjust prices to reach the product efficiency frontier in the spanish automobile market," *Omega*, 2014.

[86]   J. Meier, "Sources of Insight," 25 March 2009. [Online]. Available: http://sourcesofinsight.com/4-stages-of-market-maturity/. [Accessed 04 07 2014].

[87]   A. Martinez and R. Haddock, "The Flatbread Factor," *Strategy and Business*, vol. 46, p. 66, 2007.

[88]   R. M. Warner, Applied statistics: From bivariate through multivariate techniques, Sage, 2008.

[89]   H. Abdi, "The Kendall rank correlation coefficient," *Encyclopedia of Measurement and Statistics.*, pp. 508-510, 2007.

[90]   P. Wessa, "Free Statistics Software, Office for Research Development and Education, version 1.1.23-r7," 2014. [Online]. Available: http://www.wessa.net/. [Accessed 04 10 2014].

[91]   C. R. Whiting, "2012-13 Football Rivalry Survey Results," 28 08 2012. [Online].   Available: http://thechriswhitingshow.wordpress.com/2012/08/28/2012-football-rivalry-census-results/. [Accessed 01 08 2014].

[92]   A. Ritter, C. Cherry and B. Dolan, "Unsupervised modeling of twitter conversations," *The 2010 Annual Conference of the North American Chapter of the Association for Computational Linguistics,* pp. 172-180 , 2010.

[93]   K. Leetaru, S. Wang and G. Cao, "Mapping the global Twitter heartbeat:

The geography of Twitter," *First Monday,* vol. 18, no. 5, 2013.

[94]   T. Guimarães, "REVEALED: The Demographic Trends For Every Social
         Network,"   21   10   2014.   [Online].   Available:
         http://www.businessinsider.com/2014-social-media-demographics-update-
         2014-9. [Accessed 24 10 2014].

[95]   H. Karau, Fast Data Processing with Spark, Packt Publishing Ltd, 2013.

[96]   K. Gimpel, N. Schneider, B. O'Connor, D. Das, D. Mills, J. Eisenstein, M.
         Heilman, D. Yogatama, J. Flanigan and N. A. Smith, "Part-of-Speech
         Tagging for Twitter: Annotation, Features, and Experiments," in
         *Proceedings of the 49th Annual Meeting of the Association for
         Computational Linguistics: Human Language Technologies: short papers-
         Volume 2,* 2011.

[97]   . V. N. Khuc, C. Shivade, R. Ramnath and J. Ramanathan, "Towards
         building large-scale distributed systems for twitter sentiment analysis," in
         Proceedings of the 27th Annual ACM Symposium on Applied Computing,
         2012.

[98]   V. Perez-Rosas, C. Banea and R. Mihalcea, "Learning Sentiment Lexicons
         in Spanish.," in *LREC,* 2012.

[99]   R. Remus, U. Quasthoff and G. Heyer, "SentiWS-A Publicly Available
         German-language Resource for Sentiment Analysis.," in *LREC,* 2010.

[100]   U. Waltinger, "GermanPolarityClues: A Lexical Resource for German
         Sentiment Analysis," in *LREC,* 2010.

[101]   B. O'Connor, R. Balasubramanyan, B. R. Routledge and N. A. Smith, "From
         tweets to polls: Linking text sentiment to public opinion time series," in
         *Proceedings of the International AAAI Conference on Weblogs and Social
         Media,* Washington, DC, 2010.

[102]   The Oxford English Dictionary, Oxford University Press, 2001.

[103]   B. Gonçalves, N. Perra and A. Vespignani, "Modeling users' activity on twitter networks: Validation of dunbar's number," *PloS one,* vol. 6, no. 8, 2011.

[104]   Wolfram Alpha LLC—A Wolfram Research Company, "Wolfram|Alpha: Computational   Knowledge   Engine,"   [Online].   Available: http://www.wolframalpha.com/. [Accessed 07 10 2014].

www.ingramcontent.com/pod-product-compliance
Lightning Source LLC
LaVergne TN
LVHW092338060326
832902LV00008B/715